John Ralph Lawrenson, 54, was until 1971 one of Reuters' most senior executives in charge of a third of the company's business. He joined the news agency in 1954 as one of its first graduate trainees and spent four years in South East Asia. After a year in Southern Africa he was transferred to Latin America where, with a gap of a year, he was in charge of the continent for over four years. He returned in 1967 to become the European manager for the economic services. As a foreign correspondent he has reported nearly every kind of news event including revolutions and earthquakes, diplomatic conferences and even the last world football championship before the advent of live television. He set up the first successful Spanish language service for Latin America and has also travelled extensively selling commercial services and organising new ones throughout Africa. He likes to describe himself as a millionaire – in miles travelled – and now runs his own business newsletter publishing company from a former rectory in Suffolk.

Lionel Barber is a financial journalist and a former Young Journalist of the Year (1981). He has spent his whole career in newspapers, specialising in business and political journalism on *The Scotsman* and *The Sunday Times*. His publications include *The DeLorean Tapes* and a contribution to *The Scottish Government Yearbook* (1981). He has recently joined the staff of the *Financial Times*. He spent three months during 1985 as the Lawrence Stern Fellow at the *Washington Post*.

The Price of Truth

The story of the REUTERS £££ millions

JOHN LAWRENSON & LIONEL BARBER

SPHERE BOOKS LIMITED
London and Sydney

First published in Great Britain by
Mainstream Publishing Company (Edinburgh), Ltd 1985
Copyright © John Lawrenson & Lionel Barber, 1985, 1986
Revised edition published by Sphere Books Ltd 1986
30–32 Gray's Inn Road, London WC1X 8JL

Set in 10 on 12pt Linotron Times

Printed and bound in Great Britain by
Collins, Glasgow

CONTENTS

To
The anonymous reporter

'Set a watch O Lord, upon our
tongues that we may never
speak the unkind word that
is untrue, or being true is only
half the truth, or being wholly
true is merciless'

Attributed to 'Rufous' Bruce-Lockhart

FOREWORD

As any editor knows, the problem with a news story is not finding enough material but deciding what to leave out. This story is no exception, Many of those who have contributed to the Reuters story over the years are not named here, not because their contribution was insignificant but because it did not add to the theme of the book.

The authors would like to acknowledge the help given by past members of Reuters who included Gerald Long, Sir Christopher Chancellor, Brian Stockwell, Dominick Jones, Doon Campbell, Patrick Seale, Brian Horton, Jonathan Fenby, Max Bouckalter, Cromarty Bloom, Vernon Morgan, Robert Elphick and Harold King. It should be stressed that the authors had no access to any Reuters archives although individuals working for the company, who cannot be named, were most helpful.

We would also like to thank two past members of the news agency, Alfred Geiringer and Ian Fraser, and Brian Whitaker of the *The Sunday Times*, who provided valuable comments on an early draft. Past chairmen of Reuters and the Press Association, Sir John Burgess and Malcolm Graham, respectively, were most helpful. Special mention must go to Sir Richard Storey who made available the papers collected by his father, Lord Buckton, during the short period he was chairman of Reuters. Graham Storey's official history of the news agency, *Reuters' Century*, was a valuable source of information.

To David Leppard goes our thanks for his ferreting in the Foreign Office files at Kew, his persistence in digging out what seemed for long to be permanently hidden, and his production of the Index.

The book would not have been possible without the encouragement of Caroline Lawrenson who processed each word, and the invaluable guidance and constructive criticism of Frank Barber.

J.R.L., L.B.

THE GATHERING OF THE CLANS

'It was as if we had all discovered oil at the bottom of the garden.'
—Lord Hartwell, owner of the Daily Telegraph Group.

In the fourth floor newsroom of Reuters news agency in London the duty editor checked the 1000 GMT summary: a new Iranian offensive near Basra, a West German loan for the Siberian gas pipeline, a thirty-day state of emergency in Peru. The morning of July 14, 1982, was going smoothly, just another routine shift at 85 Fleet Street. An hour later the filing editor was pressing the transmit key for the world news schedule ('the sked') that alerted foreign editors in Europe to what Reuters judged to be the big stories for the next morning's papers. At 11.06 the automatic data exchange was logging the last of seventeen datelines.

It was around noon that the first signs appeared to suggest that the day could well prove to be anything but routine for Reuters and the newspaper world. The first of a select group of businessmen with a marked lack of enthusiasm for publicity were beginning to cross the pavement to enter the Lutyens-designed Portland stone building which is Reuters' worldwide headquarters: Lord Hartwell of the *Daily Telegraph*, Lord Rothermere of the *Daily Mail*'s Associated Newspapers, senior executives of the *Guardian*, the Express Group, the *Observer*, and Mirror Group Newspapers. For the first time, so far as anyone could recall, the barons and liegemen of the Fleet Street press were gathering under the roof of the world's most famous news agency. The Reuters building is just about a mile from the banks, brokerage and finance houses of the City of London, but on that day the agency was being drawn a whole lot closer.

It was Lord Marsh, the former Labour Cabinet Minister and chairman of British Rail, who had smoothed the way for this secret meeting between Reuters senior management and the Fleet Street shareholders. Marsh had long since dropped his socialist pretensions, preferring to seek a more rewarding career in company boardrooms. His skill as a mediator, blessed with a certain amount of political cunning, had singled him out as the right man for the newspaper industry's bed of nails: the chairmanship of the umbrella organisation for Britain's national press, the Newspaper Publishers' Association, which has to live with an army of trade unions often stigmatised as the most rapacious in the land.

Ostensibly, the NPA is the grand forum for the national newspaper proprietors to discuss the problems of the industry. It is based in a plain building at 6 Bouverie Street, just two minutes' walk from Reuters' headquarters, with the *Sun* and *Daily Mail* to the south and the *Telegraph* and *Express* to the north in Fleet Street. Surrounded geographically, it has found itself all too often caught in the middle of the warring factions among its own members, many of whom appear to detest each other. Over the years, its influence has declined to the point where many of the proprietors have ceased to take it seriously. The monthly Council meetings are almost invariably badly attended, with most proprietors preferring to send their senior managers rather than risk having to sit round the same table with rival publishers. Indeed, as Marsh has been heard to say, it is often impossible to contact a proprietor, let alone persuade him to come to Bouverie Street.

July 14 was no exception. Though the meeting had been flagged for weeks in advance, Marsh was still mising at least three top proprietors and some newspapers were not even represented. It was a frustrating experience for Marsh. Some three months before, through the NPA's representatives on the Reuters board, he had heard rumours that the agency was preparing to pay a dividend to shareholders, the first for forty-one years. On May 11, the £1.9 million pay-out was confirmed officially, the result of a leap in profits in the previous year, 1981, when earnings had quadrupled to more than £16 million. This year, the forecasts were even better, with profits of more than £35 million on the cards. The rumour was that Reuters was the source of enormous wealth; and the British national press, as part owners of the agency, stood to gain a substantial and completely unexpected windfall. If only they could agree among themselves.

Marsh, in six years in the NPA chair, had hardly spared a thought for his newspaper members' 41 per cent shareholding in Reuters: the subject had never been raised and he, like his members, had not regarded the shares as being in any way valuable.[1] These, held in trust by the NPA, were pieces of paper gathering dust in the vaults beneath the Bouverie Street building. Only when the £1.9 million pay-out was announced by Reuters did Marsh decide to investigate.

Reuters' financial resurrection can be summed up in one word:

2

Monitor. This was the code word* which the agency used to launch a computerised business and financial data service in 1973. Ten years later, Monitor was contributing 89 per cent of the agency's revenues and almost all of its pre-tax earnings.[1]

The Reuter Monitor Service is, in many ways, merely an adaptation of the basic business launched 134 years ago by the agency's founder, Baron Julius de Reuter. He, too, had started up by supplying financial information. In 1849, the former Berlin bookseller spotted that financiers in the commercial centres of Berlin and Paris were isolated from each other because of a gap in the new European telegraph service between Brussels and Aachen. His solution: carrier pigeons. Reuter had recognised their use while working for Charles-Louis Havas, a Frenchman who created one of Europe's first news bureaux in Paris, using the birds to carry information from capital to capital. Reuter's own pigeons could cover the Brussels-Aachen gap in two hours, seven hours faster than the mail train. It was a brilliant success until the business was grounded by the completion of the telegraph.

More than 100 years later, the Reuter Monitor Service filled a similar gap in the financial information market. Exploiting the technology of the micro-chip, it provided a super-fast, easy-to-use information base for money traders and financiers around the world. Until then, they had relied on the telephone and telex, by comparison a primitive and inefficient system. The Monitor service allowed currency dealers to tap their own exchange rates on desk-top terminals, while simultaneously viewing the rates of competitors on their own video screens.

The new service was launched at a particularly favourable time. For almost thirty years the exchange rates of the world's major currencies had been fixed under the Bretton Woods agreement. In 1971, President Nixon, for domestic reasons, floated the US dollar off the fixed rate of $35 an ounce for gold and Bretton Woods collapsed. Trading in currencies in the world's exchange houses in London, New York, Tokyo and Hong Kong soared. The Arab oil embargo two years later made the currency markets even more volatile. Increasingly, businessmen and financiers realised that they would have to play the currency casino if they were not to be caught out by fluctuating exchange rates in their international markets. By 1983, the agency's rapidly expanding and varied

* According to Reuters, the name derived from the mythical goddess Juno Moneta who gave her name to money since her temple in Rome later housed the city's mint. However, the more likely derivation is the Latin *monere* 'to warn'.

financial services had more than 15,000 subscribers in 112 countries and carried quotes on 106 currencies, more than 135 commodities, 37,000 stocks and 3,000 bonds, as well as information on coins, precious metals, and the availability of and requirements for oil tankers and dry cargo vessels around the world. When two years before, the Monitor Service was refined to allow subscribers to 'talk' to each other direct through the system and fix deals within minutes, the agency's profits lifted off.

Reuters' astonishing turnaround had left its hareholders in Fleet Street standing. Across the road from the agency's headquarters, the *Daily Express* and the *Daily Telegraph* were still stuck with the old linotype machines which spat out metal for a printing process which had barely changed in seventy years. The same was true of Reuters' other main shareholder, Britain's domestic news agency, the Press Association. Collectively owned by the provincial press in Britain, the PA too had failed to move into the computer age. PA journalists were still bashing out their stories on typewriters, while their Reuter counterparts were writing and editing thousands of words daily on video display units, ready to flash them directly to subscribers' video screens, teleprinters and their computer memories around the world. It is one of Fleet Street's great ironies that both these news agency organisations could be housed in the same building, a peaceful if incongruous coexistence.

The gap in financial and technological strength between Reuters and its shareholders was a relatively recent phenomenon. The agency had seen dark days itself. In 1941, when the City of London was sent up in flames by the German Luftwaffe, Reuters lurched perilously close to bankruptcy. The costs of sustaining an extensive reporting network across the globe had placed an intolerable strain on the company's finances, even before war broke out in 1939. Two years later, as the conflict engulfed Europe, South-East Asia and Africa, the agency's operations were in jeopardy. The British Government, only too well aware of the enormous value to the war effort of London being the headquarters of a worldwide news agency with an acknowledged reputation for integrity and truth-telling, was determined not to see it go under. Winston Churchill, aided by his confidant Brendan Bracken, persuaded the national newspapers to bail out the agency by taking up shares. At the same time, a Trust agreement was signed by the participants in the rescue package pledging to protect Reuters' independence and freedom from bias. It was, as we shall see, a brilliant public relations exercise which obscured the close relationship between

Reuters and the government of the day. But it secured the future of the agency, and it served its purpose in the post-war expansionist phase of the company's history.

Even the most charitable view of Fleet Street's post-war ownership of Reuters would describe it as one of indifference. Ignorance of the agency's burgeoning financial services was paralleled by a lukewarm attitude to the news service. There were constant gripes about the level of subscription fees; and despite the agency's fine reputation for fast, accurate and impartial reporting, there were suspicions that some proprietors regarded it as an expensive luxury. Reuters might still be the first with the news, such as the world scoop of Khruschev's historic denunciation of Stalin before the 20th Party Congress in 1956, but the amount of space its reports could command in an increasingly entertainment-oriented national press was shrinking fast.

There were, however, certain hidden benefits for the agency's NPA shareholders. For instance, their 41 per cent holding allowed them to nominate three directors to the Reuters board. The posts carried enormous prestige abroad, where the agency's reputation was even higher than in its British base. Its long-standing international presence, coupled with its steady unsensational reporting, compelled respect; and the acclaim rubbed off on Reuters' directors. As one senior NPA man remarked: 'Anywhere you went in the world, the chauffeur-driven Rolls was likely to be waiting for you at the airport.'

For Reuters' part, the relationship with its shareholders had one single appeal: a lack of interference. The purpose of the Trust agreement of 1941 had been to protect the agency's independence and therefore its integrity as a news medium. In this respect, it succeeded because neither the PA nor the NPA sought to massage the news flowing through the Reuters wire service. Nor did they seek to interfere in the day-to-day running of the business or to stand in the way of the shift towards more economic news in the early 1960s. When the decisions on investing millions of pounds in computers came up, there was plenty of debate in the Reuters boardroom and more than the occasional attack of nerves. But in most respects, they left the management alone. By 1982, both management and shareholders could reflect that this was one shotgun marriage which had stood the test of time.

The rumours of the £1.9 million dividend set off a flurry of interest in the agency's affairs. By July 14, when the meeting was held, most of the NPA's members knew there was more to Reuters than a ticker-tape news service, though they had only a glimmering of the true state of affairs. Two men who were better informed

5

were Rupert Murdoch, the Australian newspaper magnate with publishing interests on three continents, in Australia, the United States, and Britain; and Alan Hare, managing director of the *Financial Times*, a part of the Pearson Longman publishing and banking empire. Both men were Reuters directors and were well aware of the catalytic effect of the dividend on the value of their own shareholding.

For Murdoch, who had only recently bought the troubled and loss-making Times Newspapers operation from the Canadian Thomson family, the Reuters shares offered the prospect of mouthwatering windfall dividends. But there was a more challenging thought which occurred to the fast-thinking Australian. What if a market value could be placed on the Reuters shares by turning the news agency into a public company? With Reuters' management forecasting breakneck growth in the next three years, thanks to the success of the Reuter Monitor Service, the resulting figures would be, in his words, 'mind boggling'.

Such thoughts, had they been uttered publicly at this stage, would have provoked an outcry. Reuters was a national institution, as British as roast beef and warm beer. Besides, as Murdoch was soon to learn, the 1941 Trust agreement was to provide a formidable obstacle to a quick killing cashing in his Reuters' chips.

When the agency was rescued in 1941 by the national newspapers, safeguards had been laid down to protect it against unwelcome bidders. The most important was that the shareholders were severely restricted in their ability to sell their shares, since they were held in trust by the NPA. Moreover, the Trust agreement of 1941 laid down that the shareholders in Reuters should consider their holding 'in the nature of a trust rather than an investment'. Indeed, the appointment of ten trustees to oversee the agreement made it doubly difficult to see how shareholders could cash in their shares or tamper with them in any way without breaking the Trust agreement.

What few people realised was that secret discussions about turning the agency into a public company had been going on for at least six months before the July 14 meeting. Though strictly informal, they were nonetheless deadly serious. The key figures involved were Alan Hare, Rupert Murdoch and a former Reuters journalist and top City financier, Ian Fraser.

Fraser's connection with Reuters went back more than thirty-five years. An Oxford-educated linguist with a distinguished war record as a lieutenant in the Scots Guards, Fraser had joined Reuters in 1946 as a correspondent, gaining his first posting at twenty-three in Allied-occupied Germany. His fluent command of German and his succinct reporting marked him out as a high flier. Sent to Berlin, he made numerous useful contacts and acquaintances, including a fleeting one with a precocious Czech by the name of Robert Maxwell, at that time engaged in a lively trade in books and documents from the archives in the Russian sector, now East Berlin. Many years later, Fraser and Maxwell's paths would cross again, Fraser as the director-general of the City of London's Takeover Panel and Maxwell as the pugnacious chairman of Pergamon Press fighting a losing battle to save his business reputation.

By 1956, Fraser was chief correspondent in Germany. He had watched a nation on its knees become a major economic force on the Continent, despite the unnatural division of the country between East and West; he had gained management experience running a news bureau; and he had struck up what was to be a lifelong friendship with another Reuters high-flier, Gerald Long. The two men shared a common love for languages, with Fraser's German a match for Long's French. Each respected the other's ability, a sign perhaps that they both believed they would make it to the top. It was a source of some regret, therefore, when Long heard that Fraser had decided to abandon journalism to pursue a career in the City of London with the up-and-coming merchant bank SG Warburg. As Fraser moved up, he introduced Reuters to Warburg's and the subsequent deal made the bank the agency's primary financial adviser.

Long rose rapidly through the reporting ranks before moving into management and, in 1963, assuming the top job of chief executive. It was he, more than anyone else, who was to drive the agency forward into the computer age. It was a task which the abrasive and somewhat truculent Long relished, stamping his authority on the agency's affairs and giving short shrift to those who doubted the wisdom of the move into business and financial data services. As he said, remarking on his relations with the board at the time: 'I took the attitude, you have appointed me. I recommend this. If you don't want it – fire me.'

Through his friendship with Long, Fraser was able to keep in touch with the agency's affairs at a time when it was undergoing its greatest changes. It put him in a unique position. For more than any other person outside the board and the management, Fraser came to understand and appreciate the switch in emphasis towards financial services. By the time the Reuter Monitor Service had begun to take off in the late 1970s, the journalist/banker had come to the conclusion that the agency had changed fundamentally in character. No longer was it a straightforward news agency living from hand to mouth on subscriptions; it had become a world force in a new and lucrative market. The question was whether the agency in its present form and constitution was capable of assuming the leading role that beckoned in the information technology age.

In 1980 – when is unclear – Fraser met Gerald Long and argued plausibly that if Reuters was to realise its full potential it would need to draw on enormous resources. Having been appraised of the difficulties Long had encountered in the late 1960s, when the first wave of big investments in computer technology were called for, he said that it was no longer realistic to think of the agency financing growth out of its own revenues. The sums, this time round, would be simply too huge to handle. Moreover, Reuters no longer enjoyed the technological lead over its competitors of ten years before; others had grasped the need for computer-based systems to allow the money traders, the banks and the brokers to 'talk' to each other to conclude deals. In an increasingly competitive market, smaller rivals such as the American firm Telerate were nibbling away at Reuters' market share. Sooner or later, there was the risk that the really big American multinationals such as IBM would enter the game and upset all of Reuters' fancy growth forecasts. As a financial man with nearly twenty-five years' experience in the City of London and more than nine directorships under his belt, including the chairmanship of the merchant bank Lazards, Fraser reckoned the conclusion was inescapable: Reuters would need to tap the stock market for the necessary funds, and that meant turning the agency into a fully-fledged public company. But he advised that the time was not yet ripe; the Trust arrangements were so complex that virtually every proprietor had a right of veto and the innate conservatism of Fleet Street was such that they would not agree on a course of action until they could see the financial benefit at close quarters. Fraser recommended waiting until the profitability was really proven.

Long did not disagree with Fraser's view of the future. As he was to remark later: 'The logic of everything I did was to make Reuters a normal commercial company.'[4] But, after seventeen years at the helm, he was not the same man Fraser had known in the old days. He had spent little time with his family and not enough in his beloved France. The stocky parade ground sergeant-major figure, with his closely cropped hair and his bristling moustache, had grown weary of belting out orders to the troops in the field. He had lost momentum, and instinctively he knew that he was not the man to oversee the radical changes suggested by

Fraser. He believed that the last service to perform for a company or organisation was to leave it at the right time; he confided to friends that he was horrified at the idea of hanging on in the top job. By 1980, he cut a lonely figure in his seventh floor office at Reuters in Fleet Street, sitting and waiting for a new challenge.

The clean, quick exit Long wanted came unexpectedly after a Reuters board meeting on December 10, 1980. Rupert Murdoch took him aside and told him that he was thinking of bidding for Times Newspapers. Murdoch, who had joined the Reuters board a year before, asked Long to become his managing director at *The Times*. Long needed a three-second pause before answering 'Yes'. As he later told Harold Evans, then editor of *The Sunday Times* and soon to become the editor of *The Times*, 'The combination of *The Times* and Rupert is irresistible.'[5] In the event, both Evans and Long were to find their new partnership with Rupert Murdoch highly combustible and less than durable.

Gerald Long left his post with a Reuters-paid flat in Paris and a portrait of Baron Julius Reuter, whose maxim 'Follow the Cable' had always seemed to Long the basic lesson in running the business. Long's own management achievement was to have built up a nucleus of top managers who had stayed with the company throughout its great transformation over the past twenty years. Nigel Judah, about to be appointed finance director, Michael Nelson, the general manager, and Glen Renfrew, the head of the agency's North American operations, formed a highly talented coterie of top executives, each with a fine understanding of the business and each in accord with Long's aims for the agency. The choice of a successor was settled quickly and fell to Renfrew.

On the surface, he was not a natural choice. In his early days, he had been a bit of a wild boy. Fresh off the boat from Australia, he received almost universally bad reports from every section of the agency's commercial services he visited during the first trial months. One department head was heard to explode 'Get rid of him' after the Australian had cruised through his section. Renfrew went on to spend nine years in a variety of management posts in Southern Africa, South-East Asia (where he was pulled out sharpish after giving a senior colleague a black eye), Belgium and the United States. His big promotion came in 1964 when he took charge of Reuters' newly established computer services. He spent six years in the job, assuming worldwide responsibility for the products which were at the nerve centre of Reuters' expansion programme in the 1960s. In 1971, he took charge of the company's operations in North America, a key area after the decision by Long to abandon the once cosy relationship with the American news agency, AP, and compete head-on in the US market. His success singled him out as a possible successor to Long, although it meant leapfrogging the *de facto* number two Michael Nelson.

When he took over as managing director, Renfrew set out to realign the agency's financial affairs. The first clues came after a board meeting on December 9, 1981, which approved a more specific statement on the company's objectives set out in the 1941 Trust agreement, by which the company's owners undertook to ensure that 'Reuters shall not pass into the hands of any interest, group or faction, that its integrity, independence and freedom from bias shall be preserved, and that no effort shall be spared to expand, develop and adapt the business of Reuters in order to maintain its position as the world's leading news agency'.[6]

Renfrew's amendment was that, Reuters, from now on, would be committed to seeking to 'maintain and enshance its position as the world's leading news agency organisation *and supplier of electronic information services*' (authors' italics). Two paragraphs emphasise 'the importance of technological advance and financial services', coupled with a stirring call for 'not just profitability but for substantial profits'.

Renfrew went on to send what was a prophetic message to staff: 'In the course of raising our sights for Reuters business and deciding to aim not just for profitability but substantial profits, we have occasionally been asked how we justify the call for higher profits. Why the question goes, when we look like beginning to make reasonable profits, do we try to make more? The question, I believe, typifies an attitude which is fortunately rare in Reuters but which, if allowed to take hold, could destroy any company. We cannot afford to stand still or go slowly. We are faced with strong and growing competition in the markets from which we earn most revenue. Companies with much greater resources than our own are preparing to enter these markets . . . Substantial rising profits are the only guarantee that we shall be able to defend ourselves and prosper.'[7]

These comments were the clearest public indication yet that Renfrew was well aware of the challenge spelt out by Fraser for the company's future. But there was no suggestion at this stage that either Renfrew or his senior colleagues, Nelson and Judah, had accepted the Fraser diagnosis of turning Reuters into a public company. Nelson is adamant that going public was neither discussed nor even contemplated at this juncture.[8] Indeed, Renfrew's message to staff was quite specific in repeating what had been the company's philosophy towards expansion, that it should be met by the generation of cash internally. If Reuters was going to be cash flush in the next three to five years (profits were expected to treble to £50 million in 1983–4), then there was no obvious need to call on the market for money. Or so the argument went.

Nevertheless, Reuters' senior executives, led by Renfrew, had drawn one lesson from these spectacular profit figures. Two months before the communiqué to staff, the board had accepted a proposal almost certainly from Renfrew,[9] that the new ruling management triumvirate should be allowed to buy newly issued shares in the agency. These new 'E' shares were a special class of shares with restrictions on trading similar to the ones held by the national newspapers, and there was a tacit acceptance that other senior employees would be able to buy shares if the agency's fortunes continued to rise. It all seemed an innocuous move at the time, ample reward for the men who had contributed so much to Reuters' success over the past twenty years. Few spared a thought for Gerald Long who by this time was fighting fires in his new job at Times Newspapers. His Paris flat looked a little less attractive now that his one-time colleagues held shares which had turned them into paper millionaires.

Though Reuters' own management appeared, at this stage, to have ruled out any chance of the agency going public, the informal discussions among directors had begun in earnest. Renfrew's three-year plan and the disclosure of profit forecasts concentrated minds, above all in the case of Alan Hare, the managing director of the *Financial Times*.

Hare, as the editor of the *Financial Times* Geoffrey Owen once wrote, is famous for his long sentences, the structure of which is sometimes difficult to discern. He seemed, at first sight, rather too gentle for the rough and tumble of the newspaper business, but he brought an aristocratic touch to the Reuters board. Born the fourth son of the Earl of Listowel, he was educated at Eton and New College, Oxford. During the Second World War, he volunteered for service in the Special Operations Executive and was parachuted behind enemy lines in Albania, where he fought with the partisans for more than a year. After the war, he was rumoured to have continued his work for the British secret service. On the face of it, he seemed ideally suited for the clandestine operation to win support for turning Reuters into a public company.

It was Ian Fraser who, at this early stage, pulled the strings. He knew Hare well through his many directorships in the Pearson empire which owned the *Financial Times*. Indeed, as chairman of Lazards and a director of S. Pearson and Son, he could be fairly said to have had a direct interest in Reuters going public. Though the Pearson 5 per cent stake in Reuters was by no means as great as other national newspaper groups. Pearson's could not fail but benefit financially.

Hare became a quick convert to Fraser's arguments and agreed to sound out other directors.[10] The trouble was guessing which ones were likely to prove sympathetic. The first director he spoke to was Rupert Murdoch, who was at the time preoccupied with Times Newspapers. Print union disputes and stoppages had pushed the company deep into the red, just months after he had assumed ownership. He listened with interest, but remained non-committal. Hare then approached Tony Miles, the old-fashioned tabloid journalist who was editorial director of Mirror Group Newspapers. Miles too was non-committal, unsure of the figures and uncertain how far he should be involved.

Sometime in the spring of 1982, no one within the board is prepared to say precisely when, the matter of Reuters going public was raised for the first time. Renfrew and his colleagues listened to Hare's proposal with mounting unease. It meant a break with the past after forty years of benevolent ownership. It was a leap into the unknown for the shareholders and Reuters' own management. It opened up too a mistrust between the shareholders and Reuters' top men who feared that the agency was about to be plundered. But there was, after all, a glittering pot of gold apparently within reach of all concerned. Renfrew refused to be drawn on his own opinions, saying that it was a matter for shareholders.[11] The meeting broke up, with each participant swearing to secrecy lest the news leak out.

Outside the Reuters boardroom, there was plenty of rumour and counter-rumour fed by the public announcement of the dividend. A prescient article in the *Guardian* about Reuters' share certificates being worth a fortune, suggested that someone had been doing a bit of discreet briefing. By May, the Newspaper Publishers' Association, led by Lord Marsh, was on the scent and the first requests for a meeting had been received by the Reuters management. It was becoming increasingly difficult to ward off inquiries and so the July 14 meeting was arranged for the Fleet Street shareholders.

The July meeting, in the Reuters boardroom on the seventh floor of the agency's headquarters, lasted two and a half hours, a good deal longer than anyone had expected. Renfrew, Nelson and Judah took those present through the company's post-war success story and answered a succession of questions. As this meeting drew to a close, Lord Marsh cast a glance round the room. He saw the expression of certain shareholders tighten as they realised for sure that they were sitting on a goldmine.

RAIDERS OF THE LOST ARK

'My first motive is always profit. Let us get that quite straight.'
—Victor Matthews, on the launch of *Daily Star*.

The small group of men who coveted Reuters millions were often spoken of as the Fleet Street press barons. But they were pale shadows of the barons of the past. Those men had run their fiefdoms after a fashion that would not have been out of place in mediaeval England. When proprietors such as Rothermere of the *Daily Mail* or Beaverbrook of the *Daily Express* launched their crusades, the staff followed in train, bound, as it were, by feudal loyalty. Those were the men who had, in the darkest days of the Second World War and at the behest of Winston Churchill, taken the pledge to maintain the independence and integrity of Reuters news agency. Now, forty years on, only one of the names on the 1941 Trust agreement was still heard in the Street: Rothermere, and he was the son of the wartime Rothermere. Otherwise, Fleet Street was filled with strangers, and only one had the Street-wise panache and bravado of the old-time barons: Rupert Murdoch. His rivals were more often than not tycoons who fancied the notion of owning a newspaper.

These new newspaper proprietors were surrounded by almost as many myths as its old ones had been. They were supposed to keep their eyes firmly on the bottom line. They would deal ruthlessly with any publication, no matter its history or tradition, which failed their strict tests of profitability. They would refuse to hobnob with the mighty, the cause of the downfall of their imperious predecessors. Above all, they would stamp out the ruinous working practices which threatened the very existence of Fleet Street as the home of the national newspaper industry.

Victor Matthews, fifty-eight when he arrived in the Street after a string of successes with the Stowe-educated Nigel Broackes in property deals, construction and shipping, was reassured by the thought that his background could give him an advantage in dealing with the print unions. Schooled in the language of the building site, Matthews could out-Billingsgate the rough-tongued publisher Robert Maxwell. Matthews was a patriot born and bred as only a working-class lad can be. On his first day in the chairman's seat at the *Daily Express*, he let it be known that he was as well equipped as his predecessor – the Canadian Max Beaverbrook, The Beaver – to carry on the Rule Britannia tradition of the newspaper, with its St George Cross set square against the masthead.

When the editors of his new titles – the London *Evening Standard*, the *Daily Express* and the *Sunday Express* – sought to extract from their new master his political philosophy, they were treated to a succession of political homilies: 'We have not got an empire anymore, but we have got Britain.' 'If believing in Britain means being Conservative, then that is what we will be.' As to Matthews' ideas about sound journalism, they came down to this: 'Porn is the easy way; that is not for us.'[1]

At the outset, Broackes gave Matthews three years to haul the Express Group into profits. Within eight weeks of his arrival in Fleet Street, it looked a distant target. Maintenance engineers, many of them casual workers, launched a claim for pay parity with the top earners, the National Graphical Association linotype operators, many of whom were earning up to £250 a week. Matthews refused and locked them out.

After a week the men agreed to withdraw their demands and negotiate new manning agreements. The first showdown with the unions – though with the weaker engineering workers – had turned into a triumph, and Matthews was soon proclaiming it as heralding a new age of realms in the national newspaper industry. In the event it proved short lived.

Matthews was later to reflect that he had never encountered trade unions more obstinate, bloody-minded and rapacious than those in Fleet Street. Though the *Express* did not suffer the damage inflicted on Times Newspapers, it was still vulnerable to sporadic outbreaks of unrest which halted production and made it doubly difficult for Matthews to turn the group round. Matthews reckoned his last chance to break the unions came with the arrival to power in 1979 of Margaret Thatcher. Here was someone who shared his view that the unions, more than any other group in the country, were to blame for Britain's decline and needed to be brought to heel; but when he sounded out the new Tory Prime Minister about specific laws to allow employers to lay off workers on wildcat strikes, she backed off. It was a bitter disappointment and Matthews was left musing that he, like so many proprietors before him, had been seen off by the tightly knit print unions.

In the early days, Matthews was still buoyant, claiming that

Fleet Street's problem was not that it was overmanned but that it was under-worked. He began to use the same language as the old-style proprietors when he set out on an ambitious new venture: the launch of a breezy new tabloid, the *Daily Star*.

It was to be a bare-breasted challenger – literally – to Rupert Murdoch's phenomenally successful *Sun* at the bottom end of the newspaper market. By printing the new title in Manchester, Matthews hoped to break the stranglehold of the London print unions and keep production costs under control. But competition for the down-market reader was ferocious. He told the *Sunday Telegraph* just before the tabloid's southern launch in February 1979: 'I hope the *Star* is going to be around for a long time yet, otherwise I am not going to be around either.'²

The *Star* did survive, but at a terrible cost. Losses were put at over £20 million, a result of heavy promotion and launch costs. The circulation had risen to 1.2 milion, compared to the *Sun*'s 3.6 milion and the *Mirror*'s 3.5 million. The *Express*, too, was bleeding badly, savaged by the *Sun* and the *Mirror*. Only the *Sunday Express*, steered by its Scottish editor, Sir John Junor, was turning in profits, and even its circulation was beginning to falter as its readership grew older, gracefully.

Matthews gradually began to tire of playing the newspaper baron, though when Mrs Thatcher, after her 1979 election victory, offered him a life peerage, he took it and grandly became Lord Matthews of Southgate. But he was weary of the cocktail parties and speech engagements, often being asked to speak on matters he knew nothing about. He much preferred a day at the races, watching in action the horses whose photographs filled his office desk. He confided to a friend: 'I know how to sell cruise liners, but selling myself I find embarrassing.'

In the summer of 1981, Matthews sought talks with his chairman, Broackes, at his headquarters in Berkeley Square, near London's St James'. Broackes' attitude to the *Express* publishing venture was at best ambiguous. Having made his first million in his twenties, he appeared to have become noticeably more conscious of his public image, seeking out work for such fashionable charities at the Tate Gallery and the Royal Opera House, Covent Garden. Yet he decided to divorce himself almost entirely from his new acquisition. He lent no management expertise to Matthews and rested content with his own three-year deadline for profitability.³ That summer, however, Broackes could no longer afford to distance himself from the newspaper venture. The *Express* losses were beginning to damage the parent company, Trafalgar House, already listing as a result of the collapse in liner trade and a flat

15

property market. The two men were driven to the same conclusion: either the newspaper titles would have to be sold or they would have to fight on alone. Fresh cash from Trafalgar was out of the question.

As it happened, the Conservative Government presented Matthews and Broackes with a neat way out of the impasse. New laws, just passed by Parliament, offered companies wishing to divest themselves of subsidiary businesses the chance to avoid big tax liabilities. The demerger legislation was aimed at breaking up conglomerates in the market place. Matthews and Broackes spotted that they could disengage Trafalgar from the newspaper group and float it off as a separate company with a stock market quote.

Thus Fleet Holdings came into being. To sweeten the deal for investors, the two men threw in the profitable publishing group, Morgan Grampian. Matthews also appointed a new chief executive, Ian Irvine. An accountant from Touche Ross, Irvine was to assume a key role in the Reuters story.

Few gave Fleet much hope of survival. Within weeks of its November launch, the share price was languishing at 16p. Carnivores such as Robert Maxwell and the Australian big-bid merchant Robert Holmes à Court were mentioned in the columns of the financial press as potential buyers. Though Fleet had an inbuilt protection of convertible loan stock against predators there would come a time when Fleet's vulnerability would be constant source of worry to Matthews. Though he once remarked 'by my time of life I could be better off in the Bahamas', he had his business reputation to think of. He, like every new proprietor, had come to Fleet Street to open newspapers, not to close them.

It was Rupert Murdoch who showed Matthews where to look. 'The Reuters business is very useful,' said Murdoch to Matthews, 'going to make a lot of money.'

Why did Murdoch do it? He did not have the reputation of a Cheeryble, ever out to do good for his fellow men. On the contrary. There were those who claimed to suspect that the spirit of Ned Kelly, the Australian bushranger and bandit, had entered Murdoch's soul when he went into newspapers.

Murdoch had built up an international publishing empire from the unpromising base of two titles in Adelaide and a rundown radio station in the mining town of Broken Hill. His spectacular achievement was to exploit this base, by snapping up ailing titles and swamping his rivals with a blend of sex, crime and sensationalism. By the time he arrived in London, to fight bruising takeover battles first for the *Sun* and later for the *News of the*

World, he had built up a business worth $50 million. By 1981, his fiefdom stretched across three continents, Australia, Europe and the United States. But it was in Britain that he really made his mark. In addition to his two popular newspapers, the *Sun* and the *News of the World*, Murdoch had acquired Times Newspapers, publisher of two of the world's most famous and respected titles: *The Times* and *The Sunday Times*.

The first eighteen months at Times Newspapers were one long corporate horror story. Despite management purges, the union disputes which plagued the titles of the former owners, the Canadian Thomson family, continued unabated. TV cameras became permanent fixtures outside *The Times*' headquarters at Gray's Inn Road; *Times* staff wondered why the TV reporters did not bother to pitch their tents outside the beleaguered building.

Murdoch himself became embroiled in the dispute, jetting in from New York, his corporate base, and retiring to the seventh floor of *The Times* to plot tactics with his harassed new chief executive Harold Long, the recruit from Reuters. The atmosphere was one of permanent crisis: Murdoch determined to crush the print unions' power, the print unions set on resisting the one man they knew could break them and thereby give a lead to the rest of the newspaper industry.

In March 1982, after yet another firecracker of a dispute, Murdoch rid himself of the new editor of *The Times*, Harold Evans, the former editor of *The Sunday Times*. The dispute between proprietor and editor had been simmering for several months, with Murdoch frustrated at Evans' failure to win support from his staff, and Evans angry at what he believed was undue interference in editorial freedom. For days Evans clung improbably to his desk, before making a stage-managed exit before millions of viewers watching the 10 p.m. news, a melodramatic end to a distinguished career in British newspapers.

Murdoch had weightier matters on his mind than the next day's screaming headlines. He knew that profits from his British operations – usually his group's biggest source of cash – were due to slump from £20 million to little more than £3 million. If his cash cow in Britain ran dry, then the expansion plans of News Corporation, Murdoch's international company, would grind to a halt.

It was precisely in this hour of need that the issue of Reuters going public came under serious, albeit informal, discussion among the agency's leading shareholders. Rupert Murdoch himself had an indirect but important connection with the agency. His father, Sir Keith, had been a director of Reuters, as well as a distinguished First World War correspondent and Australian newspaper proprietor. He had been a personal friend of Reuters' boss, Sir Christopher Chancellor, and had made him guardian to Rupert when the boy was up at Oxford University. Sir Keith had been a guardian of the 1941 Trust, and Murdoch, for all his rapaciousness and killer instinct, was unsure about tampering with the Trust. As one very senior Reuters executive was later to remark: 'Of all the Fleet Street proprietors, Rupert had the interests of the agency closest to heart.' On the other hand, when he did some quick financial sums, he realised that his shares in Reuters (fortuitously doubled by the recent purchase of Times Newspapers) could be worth up to £100 million.

It was characteristic of Murdoch that he left everyone guessing as to his real intentions on whether Reuters should go public or not. He certainly had doubts about agreeing to any proposal which would put money in his newspaper rivals' pockets, the inevitable consequence of seeking a stock market quotation for the agency. But the money appeared ready for the taking; and there were those who saw Murdoch's tip-off to Matthews as a deliberate move to put pressure on for a flotation.

Matthews himself was elated. With three national titles – the *Daily Express*, the *Sunday Express* and the *Daily Star* – and a joint 50 per cent stake in the *London Standard* held with Associated Newspapers, owners of the *Daily Mail*, Matthews held the single largest block of shares in Fleet Street. He reckoned that Fleet Holdings could come to be worth more than £100 million and the share price – still a sickly 16p – would soar. Selling the Reuters shares in the open market, he could pull in the money to transform Fleet into a major publishing business.

Matthews claimed little information on Reuters other than the news of the agency's £1.9 million dividend and Murdoch's tantalising remarks about future profits. Without a seat on the Reuters board, Matthews was the outsider. He had no idea how the agency operated, who was who, where the power rested and what the real financial prospects were. There was, however, one link to Reuters to which he had given little thought in the past: he was a Reuters trustee and as such a guardian of the principles of independence and integrity established after the 1941 rescue.

Appointed in 1980, Matthews was one of ten, nearly all ex-newspapermen or newspaper proprietors, charged with upholding the Trust agreement. At that moment, Matthews' last thought was that his preoccupations as chairman of a Fleet in difficulty might conflict with his duty as a trustee of Reuters.

As a trustee, Matthews received monthly news bulletins on the agency's activities, but he rarely cast more than a glance at the

18

circulars. Now they became required reading. Over the next fortnight, he and his new chief executive at Fleet, Ian Irvine, pulled out every single available document on Reuters: annual reports, the company's articles of association and the Trust agreement.

Irvine gave daily reports to his boss. At first, neither man was sure whether it was feasible for the news agency to go public. The Trust itself appeared to be the most formidable obstacle. Inside the three-page document stood clause 12, set out in 1941 and reaffirmed in 1953, that Reuters shareholders were to regard their shareholding 'in the nature of a trust rather than an investment'. How could Matthews cash in his Reuters shareholding without violating this crucial clause in the Trust?

As the two men pored over the documents, they discovered new barriers. Reuters' articles of association said that the status of the company could not change without the unanimous agreement of the shareholders. As Matthews was soon to learn, there were any number of people who could lay claim to Reuters shares and to a vote on the future of the agency. The Press Association, collectively owned by 120 publishers of British and Irish newspapers, also had a say.

At this stage, the PA was the least of Matthews' concerns. His main thought was of potential opposition within the Newspaper Publishers' Association council, the forum of the national newspaper proprietors. After five bruising years on the NPA council, he knew something of the rivalries between the barons, of which the most bitter was probably between himself and Lord Rothermere, the chairman of Associated Newspapers.

Vere Harold Esmond Harmsworth, the third Viscount Rothermere, controlled a newspaper and publishing empire which had always been the personal fief of the senior member of the Harmsworth family. The third Viscount had much to live down. His grandfather, Harold Harmsworth, was an admirer of Hitler and Mussolini in the 1930s and had backed the regime of Admiral Miklos Horthy, who was to take Hungary into war on Hitler's side. The Hungarians for their part invited the first Viscount Rothermere to seek weightier responsibilities than newspaper publishing and become King of Hungary. He declined, with thanks.

It was Rothermere, along with Lord Beaverbrook, who fought the great circulation wars of the 'thirties and led the attacks on the Prime Minister, Stanley Baldwin, prompting the retort that the *Express* and the *Mail* were 'engines of propaganda for the constantly changing policies, desires, personal wishes, personal likes and dislikes of two men. What are their methods? Their methods are direct falsehood, misrepresentation, half-truths. . . . What the proprietorship of these papers is aiming at is power, but power without responsibility – the prerogative of the harlot throughout the ages.'

The second Viscount, Esmond Rothermere, was no less an autocrat.[4] Board meetings were generally a forum for directors to agree to what he wanted. On occasions, the other directors would not even see the agenda until they arrived in the boardroom. But Esmond did strengthen the base of his business, constructing a chain of provincial newspapers stretching through Hull, Grimsby, Derby, Gloucester, Cheltenham and Swansea. They were to become one of the financial cornerstones of Associated Newspapers, though they were light years away from the ritzy glamour of Fleet Street. Above all, his main contribution to the group was to diversify away from newspapers, buying into, among other things, Canadian pulp, and eventually North Sea oil.

Vere Harmsworth became vice-chairman of Associated Newspapers in 1963, at the age of thirty-eight. For some time he lived in the shadow of his father, acquiring the nickname 'Mere' which stuck to him longer than seemed fair. In 1971, when his father resigned abruptly, he moved into the chair, eager to make his mark. The handover of authority coincided with the end of a series of highly secret talks between the *Mail* and *Express* Groups.[5] With the *Express* running two struggling dailies – the *Express* and the *Evening Standard* – and Associated's flagship, the *Daily Mail*, losing money, senior managers had tabled merger discussions. The idea was to combine the *Express* and *Mail* into a joint morning newspaper which would carve out a whole market to itself between the tabloid, down-market *Mirror* and *Sun* and the up-market dailies. In theory, the combination could look forward to 5.5 million sales, though in practice the figure was likely to be nearer 4.5 million. In addition there was talk of merging the groups' two London evening papers, the *Standard* and the *News*.

It appeared to make perfect sense: the new group could eliminate the withering competition and combine to become the biggest selling newspaper group in Britain. In the event, Associated withdrew from the deal at the last minute and the reason appeared to be a deliberate, though unspoken declaration of independence by the new man in charge, Vere Harmsworth. After spending years waiting for the top job, he liked the idea of being his own man. Beyond that, he was said to be relishing the prospect of slugging it out toe to toe with Beaverbrook at the *Express*. The hereditary battle was about to recommence.

Rothermere started well, relaunching the *Daily Mail* in tabloid form with a militantly conservative tone and strongly appealing to women. After an initial sales dip, the paper's punchy style caught on and circulation climbed to near 1.8 million. But the logic behind the 1971 merger talks did not disappear; and while Rothermere could boast of his successes at the *Mail*, he had to give way on the *Evening News*, agreeing to merge the paper with the *Standard* in 1981. It was during these discussions, a painful setback for Associated, that Vere Harmsworth, aristocrat and third generation press baron, had his first lengthy encounter with the former office boy, housebuilder, chartered surveyor and first generation press lord, Victor Matthews. Separated by style, temperament and tradition, the two men came to detest each other. Matthews was quite correct in suspecting that whatever ideas he entertained about grabbing the Reuters millions, the greatest opposition from within the press barons entourage would come from Rothermere.

During the summer of 1982, Matthews and Irvine worked non-stop on a feasible scheme to turn Reuters into a public company. Unknown to them, other shareholders were drawing up their own game plan.

Peter Gibbings was the quietest of Fleet Street managers. A barrister who began in newspapers by answering questions in an agony aunt column in the *Daily Mail*, he went into general management for Associated Newspapers, joined the *Observer* as circulation manager and was deputy managing director when he was recruited to the *Guardian* in 1967. He was a smooth-looking man, softly spoken with big friendly eyes, a lovable Labrador type. He rarely barked, but he could certainly bite. He attacked the *Guardian*'s losses by continuous cost trimming and, almost unnoticed, acquired a profitable batch of small newspapers in Surrey and Greater Manchester.

As chairman of the *Guardian* and Manchester *Evening News*, controlled by the Scott Trust, Gibbings was entitled to a seat on both the Newspaper Publishers' Association and the Press Association. Thus he was on the inside track in both the NPA and the PA.

Gibbings was faster off the mark than some of his colleagues inside the NPA. In March 1982, a long article appeared in the financial pages of the *Guardian* by an experienced financial reporter, Maggie Brown. Briefed anonymously by Gibbings, she gave the first authoritative account in the quality press of how Reuters' shareholders had found themselves sitting unawares on a potential goldmine.

She began with the Reuters share certificates, issued to share-holders after the 1941 rescue by Fleet Street. For forty-one years these bits of paper, apparently worthless, had been gathering dust in the vaults of the Newspaper Publishers' Association in Bouverie Street. No one had paid any attention to the certificates; no one had an inkling that they might become valuable. But in spring 1982, with the news of the dividend to shareholders pending, they had assumed tremendous importance. It was, she wrote, as if a hidden treasure had been discovered in the loft.

Brown's article aroused some interest in the City, particularly among the handful of brokers who specialise in newspaper stocks. Conor Fahy, a six-foot-six Irishman at the brokers Teather and Greenwood, began to make inquiries about just how valuable Reuters' and Fleet Street's shareholding might be.

Other moves were already gathering pace in City circles, prompted in part by the Lazards merchant bank chairman, Ian Fraser, now more convinced than ever that Reuters should become a public company. He approached Alan Hare, the managing director of the *Financial Times*.

On July 22, eight days after the first meeting of the press barons at Reuters, Hare wrote to the chairman of the Press Association, Richard Winfrey. Winfrey, whose father had held the top job at the Press Association before him, was shocked by its content. The letter contained a sketched outline of how to float the news agency on the stock market which, according to Hare and Fraser, protected the agency's independence. Despite the fact that he held a seat on the Reuters board, Winfrey, until the letter, had little notion of the moves to turn the agency into a public company. Besides, as the PA chairman found out later, Hare had not even bothered to inform most of the other Reuters directors. When he asked Hare why he had failed to contact, for example, the Australian representative on the board, he was told that a copy of the letter had been sent to the Australian Rupert Murdoch. As an excuse it hardly rated and was enough to take Winfrey's breath away. If there was one Reuters director whom the other Australian directors distrusted most, it was Murdoch.

When Winfrey passed Hare's letter to the Australians, led by Lyle Turnbull, chairman of the Australian national news agency, the Australian Associated Press, they were all horrified. They saw Hare's move as a Fleet Street wheeze to grab money. They reckoned it had nothing to do with their own immediate interests, nor with the long-term interests of the company.

The Hare/Fraser scheme did not go away. Over the summer months, Fraser spent weeks refining the plans and contacting shareholders informally to arrange briefing sessions at Lazards' main offices near the Barbican, doubtless with an eye to picking up the lucrative fees and considerable prestige of organising a flotation of the company on the stock market. He sought out each NPA shareholder, right down to the *Morning Advertiser*, first established as a daily newspaper in 1787 and now the brewery trade's journal.

Driven out of Fleet Street by crippling costs, the *Advertiser* had found refuge in South London, a stone's throw, one might say, from the scene of the Brixton riots of 1981. Chris Kimber, the Bermondsey-born managing director, had worked for the paper for forty years with overmanning, old hot-metal printing and some of his staff now into their seventies. Then the word came from on high – or rather from Alan Hare – there's a fortune waiting for your paper.

Back in Fleet Street, Victor Matthews, worried about the flagging share price of Fleet Holdings, called on the company's institutional shareholders which included the mighty insurance giant, the Prudential. His aim was to persuade them to stick with Fleet, rather than sell out. Matthews suggested that the group was a good deal stronger than appeared. Pressed for more information, Matthews began to talk about Reuters news agency. What he said sent Fleet's share price edging upwards. The prospects for a smooth first annual general meeting for the company on October 13 now looked good.

The AGM took place in the Victorian headquarters of the Chartered Insurance Institute in Aldermanbury in the City of London. Those who were present remember a breezy confidence among the shareholders' representatives. With profits at £3 million, Matthews could afford one of his lugubrious smiles as he rose to deliver his chairman's statement.

What followed is a matter of dispute. Matthews' opening remarks contained little that was controversial; the confidence expressed in the group's future merely reflected the mood of confidence in the audience. But when he finished speaking, he faced questions, and one of the first concerned Fleet Holdings shares in Reuters. Would the chairman care to elaborate?

Matthews now says he was not prepared for the question which he suspects was a plant.[6] He denies any forewarning of the inquiry, or that he intended to make any reference to Reuters at the AGM. If so, his answer was unusually candid.

There was a 'new look' about Reuters, he said. No longer was it having to be funded by its owners in Fleet Street. It was bursting with profits so, he revealed, he and several other national newspaper proprietors had been 'chivvying' Reuters' management to bring about a public quotation for this news agency. Asked when he thought such a public quote might take place, Matthews replied: 'Within twelve months.'

With those three words, Victor Matthews brought the full Reuters story out into the open. The cover was blown.

ARISE, SIR RODERICK

'The fact is that Reuters does control or dominate the news of the agencies throughout the world.'
—Adolph S. Ochs, publisher of the *New York Times*.

During the heated debate in 1982 over whether Reuters should go public, many ignored or deliberately forgot that the news agency had operated as a public company once before in its history. Reuters shares had been traded on the stock exchange for more than fifty years, first under its founder Julius Reuter and then under his son, Herbert. In the early years of the twentieth century, Reuter's Telegram Company was recognised internationally for the news service that carried its name. But selling news was not in itself very profitable, and so the company had diversified. By 1913, the success of the banking department led Herbert Reuter to believe that he could operate a fully-fledged bank. An eager public poured money into the new venture. Within two years this ill-conceived and highly speculative move had swallowed up the entire reserves of the parent company and jeopardised the future of the news agency. The share price plummeted from £12 to £4, and rumours swept the City that the bank was in trouble. On April 18, 1915, three days after the death of his Scottish wife, Edith, the body of Baron Herbert de Reuter was found slumped in an armchair in the summerhouse of his home in Reigate, Surrey. A revolver lay in his lap.

The suicide of Herbert Reuter left the company with no logical successor, a legacy of the autocratic style of Herbert and his father Julius. Whoever took over faced the same dilemma that had taxed Herbert: how to ensure the survival of a company whose main product was that costly and perishable commodity, news. This was the 'news dilemma', a *leitmotiv* in the company's history, and one which recurred more frequently as Reuters found itself competing increasingly against government-owned or government-subsidised news agencies.

When Julius Reuter started his news agency in London, he had yet to face these problems. He had left his native Germany in 1848 after some of his revolutionary writing had come to the attention of the authorities. Though trained in Berlin as a bookseller, Reuter developed an interest in news and communications. While in self-imposed exile in France, one of his first jobs was with the French news agency Havas. After less than a year, he tried competing with his former employer, operating from a squalid sitting room in Paris and helped only by his wife, Ida Maria. When that failed he moved back to the German border town of Aachen, sited at the start of the German cable network. Reuter spotted a gap between the end of the Belgian cable and the start of the German. He rented first pigeons then horses to bridge the gap and carry stock market prices from Brussels to Berlin. History has it that the man who suggested he move to London was Werner Siemens, later Werner von Siemens and the founder of the German telecommunications company that bears his name. Siemens was building the telegraph line along the railway which would eventually provide a fast link between Brussels and Aachen. Julius Reuter sent his wife to see Siemens and plead with him that completion of the telegraph line would ruin his business. It was Siemens who said to her: 'My dear lady, from what you tell me, your husband ought to sit in London and not in Aachen because London, with its underwater lines and cables, is the place to be.'

Siemens was so convinced he was right that he sent his younger brother Wilhelm, later to become Sir William Siemens, to open a cable factory in south London at Woolwich. When the cable gap was bridged, eight months later, Julius Reuter took Siemens' advice and moved to London, the city at the centre of European finance and communications.

The Great Exhibition of 1851 in London and the promise of the underwater cable link between France and England was the inspiration for the former bookseller. The secret was to buy information in one place, transmit it quickly by cable to another point and sell it to a number of companies and individuals at a profit. Stock market prices were a natural since it was cheaper for companies to buy the information rather than set up their own communication network. Reuter was able to tap a growing market, particularly in financial news. Stock exchange prices and exchange rates were posted publicly in the bourses round Europe and it was not long before Julius Reuter was saving companies in the City of London considerable sums, providing a service that was both reliable and fast, and also making handsome profits.

For an immigrant Jew in the middle nineteenth century, financial success did not immediately bring social recognition. Julius' active mind began to seek ways to provide news for the

London newspapers. In 1855, Gladstone repealed the stamp duty on newspapers, the 'tax on knowledge', thereby creating opportunities for cheap newspapers. The rapid build-up of profitable newspapers and the subsequent circulation wars created a demand for information rivalled only when television came of age a hundred years later. Julius eyed the amounts that newspaper proprietors were prepared to spend collecting their own news, noting, for instance, that *The Times* even had its own cross-Channel steamboat to rush continental news to the presses. Within ten years of his arrival in London, Reuter had signed up the London and provincial papers as subscribers; he had organised his own network of war correspondents during the Austro-Prussian war; and, most significant of all, he had signed the first international exchange of market prices with the French agency, Havas, and the German agency, Wolff.

But if Gladstone created an opportunity for the young Reuter, he also killed off one of his most successful ventures when he implemented Disraeli's Telegraph Act nationalising the private telegraph companies. Julius had laid his own private underwater cable between Lowestoft in Suffolk and the German island of Nordeney and, in order to raise the necessary money for the venture, floated his company on the London stock exchange in 1865. The company was amply compensated for being nationalised but its nature was already changing. The main thrust of its activities had become the provision of news for newspapers. As the Government encouraged the installation of international cables to link the distant corners of the Empire, Reuter followed the cable network with his news and price services. He carefully nurtured his Government and his social contacts, providing personal copies of key cables to Ministers and even to Queen Victoria herself. On one occasion the Queen asked for, and was given, the original cable that announced the relief of the siege of Mafeking. In due course, his persistence was rewarded and the Queen decreed that the European baronetcy he had been awarded in 1871 could 'enjoy the privileges of the foreign nobility in England'.

The success of the news service was due in no small part to its growing reputation for objectivity. At a time when newspapers carried political bias to extremes, the Reuter family business kept to the essential facts and, where possible, to the official version of events. But its very success meant an increase in the words carried and in the costs of the service.

New ventures had to be found to help bear these costs. Barred from running its own telegraph cables, the company concentrated on refining a system of telegram codes so that more and more information could be packed into fewer and fewer words. By the time the Baron retired to the Riviera in 1878, Reuters' Traffic Department included the commercial service and the private and business telegrams. In time it would also cover the telegraphic remittance business which provided the major contribution to profits.[1] Reuter's sophisticated coding was able to transmit instructions for payment of money across the world more cheaply than its banking competitors. Whether it was a £50 payment to a relative in need or gangs of Indian sugar workers in South Africa who wanted to send their earnings home, Reuter's remittance service was big and booming.[2]

The growth of the remittance business persuaded Herbert in 1913 to form the Reuter Bank as a wholly-owned subsidiary of the news agency. The new bank had an authorised capital of one million pounds, double that of its parent company. Now Julius and Herbert made mistakes but they had never committed themselves further than their own finances would permit. When a young Hungarian banker by the name of Hadjuska gained the Baron's ear and confidence and persuaded him that the banking department could be built up into an international financial empire, the business started to go wrong. Totally ignorant of banking affairs and lacking any directors to provide advice and expertise, Herbert allowed Hadjuska a free rein. Co-operation from other banks was not forthcoming: they were determined to squash this upstart before it became too serious a competitor. By the end of 1913 it was apparent the bank was more than a disaster in itself: it threatened the existence of the whole company.

The following year was one long horror story. The advertising department, another business venture doomed to failure, was attacked publicly by *The Times* for a circular which implied Reuters could offer special deals for newspaper coverage if firms placed their advertisements with the company. The resulting storm was such that the Reuters manager responsible committed suicide. The news service was damaged, too, when the chief correspondent in Japan became entangled in a political blackmail scandal. More seriously, the newspapers started complaining about the quality, volume and price of the news service they received. When World War One broke out, with its certain increase in reporting costs and its sure decline in revenue from newspapers and commercial houses on the continent of Europe, Reuters' future was bleak indeed.

The death of the Baron Herbert did nothing to allay the fears of the shareholders who flocked to Old Broad Street in the City of London when the postponed annual general meeting finally took place. The Baron had left a personal note which made it plain that it was the loss of his wife which made him commit suicide, but this was clearly not believed by the majority of those at the meeting. They blamed the company's troubles on Herbert and the manager of the bank, Hadjuska. The problem was to find a new chief executive to sort out the mess.

Reuters had always been a one-man show, run first by Julius, then by Herbert. The job of the board was largely ceremonial. The other directors knew practically nothing of how the company was organised or functioned; indeed they were once described as 'puppets of the family or in their dotage'.[3] At one point, there had been hopes that Herbert's son, Hubert, would eventually take over from his father. But Hubert was anything but a man of affairs, preferring a life dedicated to music and poetry. When war was declared, Hubert, thirty-eight, joined the Sportsmen's battalion and was posted to the Essex Regiment as a second-lieutenant. Because of his age, he was kept at the regimental depot, but he yearned for action at the front. One day he resigned his commission, went along to a second-hand clothes dealer, rented an overcoat to cover his uniform, and enlisted as a private in the Black Watch. Within a year he was killed in action in France and recommended posthumously for the Victoria Cross. The only other candidate in the family for the top job in Reuters was Hubert's dilettante cousin, Oliver. At the outbreak of war he had been living in Germany where he was imprisoned briefly before being released to move to Switzerland. Unmarried, nearly stone deaf and mentally unstable, Baron Oliver de Reuter finally died in Lausanne in January 1969.[4]

With no obvious successor in view, the board appointed a stopgap, the company secretary, Walter Bradshaw. The one person who might have helped with advice was the chief editor, Frederic Dickinson; but even he was unknown to the chairman, Mark Napier, who had spent thirty-six years as a director of the company, five of them as chairman.

Some 6,000 miles away in South Africa one man was not prepared to stay anonymous and see someone else steal the job he had coveted for years. Roderick Jones had started work as a teenage sub-editor on *The Press* in Pretoria, an obscure newspaper in the capital of the then independent republic of the Transvaal. Less than a decade before, gold had been discovered fifty miles away on the Rand, the site of the future city of Johannesburg. The scene was set for the monumental clash between the independent farming communities and the commercial interests of the British Empire.

29

Jones was well placed to act as 'stringer', or part-time correspondent for Reuters. He had to speak good Dutch to be able to work in Pretoria, the rustic capital where the President's wife still milked her own cow in the backyard.[5] His contacts were in a class of their own. On one occasion he read the Bible to the President, Paul Kruger, when the old man was ill in bed. He grew to know the young attorney, Jan Smuts, so well that Smuts later became godfather to one of Jones' children; and their friendship continued long after Smuts became a British Field Marshal and Prime Minister of South Africa.

As a Reuter stringer, Jones was the first to meet and interview Dr Leander Starr Jameson, the foolhardy nationalist who sparked off the three-year Boer War when he led a force of near 600 Rhodesian police and local volunteers to invade the Transvaal. Jones' interview at the Pretoria railway station with the captured Jameson was a big enough scoop to cement his reputation both with Reuters and with British officials in South Africa who were later to become vital to Jones' career.

The 'white man's war' in southern Africa highlighted for a new generation of newspaper readers the role of the war correspondent. Journalists were able to ride out on horseback to the battlefield to watch the slaughter through their fieldglasses and then gallop back to the nearest cable or postal station. It was a time when an eager reporter could make countless contacts as famous names arrived on the scene. Winston Churchill was captured but escaped from Pretoria to write vividly for the *Morning Post*, while his mother took care of her other son, John, in her private hospital ship anchored off Durban harbour. Dr Arthur Conan Doyle wrote his *Great Boer War* based on his experiences working in a military field hospital before he achieved literary fame as the creator of Sherlock Holmes. Another novelist, Edgar Wallace, was a junior Reuters correspondent. Household names of World War One such as Generals Haig and French came to prominence in South Africa. Lord Milner and, later, Lord Gladstone were both contacts that were to prove useful to Jones in the future. But of all the contacts that Jones made during this period the one that he was to use the most relentlessly was the gentleman and author John Buchan.

At the time of Herbert Reuter's death, Jones had been in charge of the company's affairs in South Africa for ten years. He had a close relationship with the chief editor, Dickinson, who backed his claim to become the successor to the Baron. Dickinson, however, had no direct say and so Jones, in Capetown, bombarded the stopgap manager, Bradshaw, with reasons why he should be invited to London.

His cables and letters were either not answered or met with little response. Bradshaw even kept one letter in his pocket for a month without mentioning it to the board. It was finally a letter that Dickinson wrote to Lord Gladstone, and which Gladstone passed to Reuters chairman Mark Napier, that focused attention on the eager manager in South Africa. Gladstone had recently returned to London from a successful tour as the first Governor-General of the Union of South Africa, and Dickinson guessed correctly that he might look with favour on the candidature of Jones. An invitation to London followed swiftly. The dapper little son of a Cheshire hat salesman charmed Napier, and, in September 1915, he finally got his reward: at thirty-seven the job of managing director of Reuter's Telegram Company.

Jones' family origins promised no sure path to his later fame. His father, for reasons unknown, was called AP-Jones – no connection with the American news agency whose campaign against the son was later to be so bitter. A family mystery still lingers as to whether Jones' father was separated or divorced from his mother, but it was a family decision that packed the son off at the age of sixteen to seek his fortune in South Africa.

Ambitious, tough, impatient, fastidious, a connoisseur of Burgundy and inclined to the impulsive – he was a shadowy, frightening figure to his children on the other side of the green baize door that separated their father from the kitchen quarters and the nursery.[6]

Little that is written or remembered about Roderick Jones is complimentary. A former Press Association chairman, Malcolm Graham, thought him 'an awkward little chap, very full of himself and a snob who had to create a tremendously big impression'.[7] The official Press Association history, *Reporter Anonymous*, recalls the memorable quote: 'very nearly a great man, except that he was not tall enough'. This was the man soon to be attacked by the publisher of the *New York Times*, Adolph S. Ochs, as now heading the organisation that 'control(s) or dominate(s) the news of the agencies throughout the world'.[8]

On the day that Jones took over as managing director the shares of the company dropped to their lowest level at £3-0-9, in pre-decimal currency. The first task was to reduce costs and sell off the bank that had all but sunk the firm. The public responded to the reorganisation as the shares edged up to the £6 level, only for the jobs of both Jones and the chairman, Napier, to be threatened by a sudden and unwelcome takeover offer.

The predator was Marconi's Wireless Telegraph Company. Through its subsidiary, Wireless Press, Marconi had a monopoly throughout the British Empire for information received via radio signals and used for publication. Only Marconi, for instance, could receive and distribute the German war communiqués and similar material that was of enormous interest to subscribers around the world.

Marconi planned at £10 a share bid totalling £500,000. The offer gave shareholders an immediate profit and was nearly the amount that most of them had originally paid. Many of the directors had only come in with the new money raised for the Reuter bank and were not concerned with the news agency operations. Both Jones and Napier saw that the board would be hard pressed to refuse Marconi's offer – unless a counter-bid was launched.

Over a hectic nine-week period the two men put together an offer to buy the company themselves at £11 a share. Jones persuaded the board to hedge on the Marconi offer while he worked on his own presentation. Today, in a tightly regulated market, such wheeler dealing would be illegal; indeed even at the turn of the century it was highly suspect.

When the new bid was finally revealed it contained the names of Napier, the exalted Privy Councillor and President of the British South Africa Company, Sir Starr Jameson, Lord Robert Peel and Lord Glenconner, chairman of the Union Bank of Scotland which was advancing the money.

The name of Jones, however, did not appear. At a critical board meeting on October 25, 1916, sprung by Jones at short notice, an incomplete offer set out by his own lawyers was tabled. Napier volunteered to leave the room during the discussions as he was an interested party. Jones, however, sat on as a director to discuss and vote on an offer in which he was the prime mover and a fifty per cent participant.

Just where did Jones get the money or security to bid £275,000, his stake in the bid for control of Reuter's Telegram Company? There was no family money: the Joneses had lost it all in the Glasgow bank crash. It is inconceivable he saved this sort of sum from his income in South Africa, even though he was in charge of the company's affairs there for ten years. The Baron had not been noted for his generosity as a paymaster and Jones had expensive tastes. He was Master of the Cape Hounds, he entertained his contacts well, dressed expensively and bought his hats at Lock's.

During the bid discussions between Napier and Jones, it was Napier who was concerned about the liability they were taking on if they succeeded. He was an experienced City financier and qualified barrister, well aware of the pitfalls. But Jones was adamant he knew where he could lay his hands on the money. He was so confident that he was prepared to buy all the shares himself if Napier backed down. As he boasted later: 'I had friends on whose support I could rely.'

Who were these powerful friends? Lord Milner, architect of the Boer War, was invited to take part but came round personally to say he was sorry he had to refuse. Only later did he disclose that he had been asked to join Lloyd George's War Cabinet. The clear indications are that the sort of money involved, or the promise of the necessary backing, could only have come from someone close to Jones who had deep pockets and more than a passing interest in a good press. The finger of suspicion points at the gold, diamond and land-owning conglomerate in the shape of the British South Africa Company, the founder of Rhodesia, and its chairman, the rehabilitated bounder, Starr Jameson.

After his trial in Pretoria, when he was sentenced to death, Jameson was reprieved and sent back to England. He was again tried and sentenced by a Bow Street special court to ten months in jail. Within eight years he had returned to South Africa, had become Prime Minister of Cape Colony, a baronet, chairman of the British South Africa Company founded by Cecil Rhodes (which they both nearly wrecked with their joint foolishness), and a Privy Councillor. One version even has it that it was 'Dr Jim' that Rudyard Kipling, another of Jones' friends in South Africa, is supposed to have taken as his model for his poem 'If', the tribute to the Victorian virtues.

Reuters (1916) Ltd., the new private company formed after the successful bid, showed that the outside directors, in the shape of Jameson, Glenconner and Peel, held a total of 501 shares while Napier had 498. The following year the company changed its name to Reuters Ltd. and, in March 1918, Jameson dropped out. It was surely no coincidence that Jameson's departure should coincide with a sharp rise in the company's indebtedness. The mortgages and other charges on the company's property, shown as zero, suddenly rose to over £153,000. It was not until June 1919 that Jones was allotted one share. Later that year Napier and Jones were shown publicly as equal partners with 500 shares each and Jones emerged as both chairman and managing director. At the same time, Glenconner and Peel disappeared and who should come in as directors but John Buchan and D. O. Malcolm, a director of the British South Africa Company. With the new South African contingent on the board, the company's indebtedness dropped by nearly £100,000.

Clearly Reuters was making a successful recovery. The bank had ceased to be a dangerous drain on the company's finances and was eventually sold. However, Marconi did not abandon its efforts to gain control. Indeed it represented a continuous threat, backed by the Admiralty which awarded the wartime monopoly. Marconi had been prepared to top Jones' price if Jones had offered half a chance. Its aims were frustrated 'by the information conveyed . . . collaterally from the highest quarters that such action would be against the public interest and if persisted in would be vetoed'.[10]

The suggestion that Jones had implicit government support throughout this difficult period became all the more credible when he took on an important government job. The need for effective wartime propaganda had long been recognised by the Government, but it was only in 1916 that the Foreign Office opened its own department of information. At its head emerged John Buchan, one-time private secretary to Lord Milner, Jones' lifelong ally and friend and named in 1923 as his successor in the event of Jones' premature death. Buchan asked Jones to take on the honorary job of Adviser on Cable and Wireless Propaganda. It is fair to say that Jones accepted only after great pressure, but it is striking that he saw no conflict of interest betwen advising on government propaganda and running an independent news agency.

The Germans saw it differently. They criticised their own propaganda efforts and pointed to the cunning British who they believed were far more successful at undermining enemy morale and keeping up spirits at home. They counted both British official propaganda and Reuters as one. As the influential newspaper, *Berliner Tagesblatt*, pointed out: 'Mightier and more dangerous than Fleet and Army is Reuter. We, too, must have a Ministry of Propaganda unless we are to be deprived of the fruits of our sacrifices, sufferings, and achievements.'[11]

Jones tried publicly to make a distinction between the work that he did during the mornings at Reuters and his unpaid work at the department. But the matter caused enough of a stir to provoke Mark Napier, the Reuters chairman, to write to *The Times*: 'Sir Roderick's position seems to be similar to that of others whose names may occur to you, men who patriotically have put on one side their own engagements in order to serve the State and who would be the last to be suspected of using their official positions to advance the interests of the great enterprises with which they are connected.'[12] His wartime efforts however, were of such value that within a year, in 1917, he was honoured with a knighthood. Shortly after, the owner of the *Daily Express*, Max Aitken, became a peer, taking his title, Lord Beaverbrook, from his home in New Brunswick. Beaverbrook inaugurated the much larger Ministry of Information and asked Sir Roderick to be chief executive as well as Director of Propaganda. His friend John Buchan moved over to become Director of Intelligence.

THE EMPIRE FALTERS

'The whole point is that we are tied up with three government-owned, possibly government-subsidised, propaganda services. We, a non-profit-making organisation, are tied up with three money-making organisations, and it is an unholy alliance.'
—Director of Associated Press, Oswald G. Villiard, publisher of
the *New York Evening Post*.

In August 1923, Sir Roderick Jones set out to do what neither of his predecessors in control of Reuters had ever accomplished. He embarked in the 59,000-tonne liner *Majestic* – formerly the German transatlantic liner *Bismarck* – to review the distant corners of his news empire.

What had begun with the Reuters pigeons flying the 120-mile stretch between Brussels and Aachen had become a vast and complex worldwide communications network. News was transmitted in morse code via cable links stretching across the globe. The British, through their active sponsorship of underwater cable, had established a world lead over their international competitors in communications. At the centre of this constant flow of news traffic, stood London and, through its base in the British capital, Reuters.

Reuters sold its service in five continents – with the notable exception of the United States. But this did not mean that there was a Reuters correspondent in every little town and remote outpost which gave a Reuters dateline to a Reuters story. Specific arrangements had been reached with other national news agencies. The French news agency Havas, for instance, covered South America and sent Latin American news to Reuters. In return, Havas had an exclusive contract to distribute to its Latin American clients world news obtained by Reuters. Meanwhile, Reuters had exclusive rights to sell Havas news to countries such as India, Japan, Australia and South Africa.

The Havas-Reuters agreement was paralleled by a similar reciprocal arrangement with the other main national news agency, the Associated Press of the United States. The German agency, Wolff, originally a member of the 'Big Four', had been a party to the international alliance until the end of World War One when it had been effectively confined to its domestic market in the role of a junior member, a reward for being on the losing side. The beauty of this 'news swap' was that each of the international news agencies – Havas, AP and Reuters, and Wolff when it was a full member – had a guaranteed and unopposed monopoly in specified countries while the other members incurred no costs whatsoever to obtain news reports from those countries. Their raw material was free. In short, the world was carved up between the members of an international news cartel with each member determining the price of the service it sold to its captive audience. While it lasted, it was a wonderfully cosy arrangement. Reuters, for instance, could sell its commercial services and strike several lucrative contracts to carry official statements, announcements or budget summaries as an extra service for which foreign governments paid a special fee. The problems would start when the American news agency decided to pull out of the cartel and start competing, directly, on Reuters' patch.

The first signs of strain appeared in September 1914, days after the outbreak of the First World War. As the French, Germans and British started digging their trenches in Europe, Señor Jorge Mitre sent a cable from Buenos Aires to Paris asking his regular news supplier, Havas, for the official German war communiqués. Don Jorge was a member of the powerful Mitre family which controlled *La Nacion*, one of the richest and most influential newspapers in Argentina, and, in the interests of balanced reporting, he wanted to make sure that he received news from both sides during the war. His request for German news got short shrift. 'Nous sommes Français,' ran the cable from Paris.

The Havas response suggested that Mitre would have to rely on one, obviously tainted source of news for the rest of the war. In desperation, on September 8, 1914, he cabled New York, asking if he could buy the AP news service, and through it, the German communiqués.

The cable from *La Nacion* lay in the pending file at AP's new traffic department for several days. The request posed an acute dilemma for the American news agency. If AP complied, it ran the risk of undermining the news agency alliance to which it had belonged for more than twenty years. Equally, it knew that it was not able, at this stage, to provide a news service to the whole of South America, as it might very well have to do if the alliance broke: the main international cable routes were dominated by the British, whose cable from London covered both the west and east coasts of South America. AP was effectively shut out.[1]

In the end, Mitre in Buenos Aires received what can only be termed a Latin negative: no reply. AP was not prepared to break the contractual agreements with its international partners for the sake of one newspaper in Argentina. But Mitre was not so easily beaten. In one last desperate move, he cabled the United Press Associations in New York and received an immediate positive response.

The UPA had no contractual ties with the Big Three news agencies. Already it was competing hard with AP in the growing American domestic market and badly needed its own foreign news sources. The UPA had no hang-ups about marching into South America. In retrospect, the decision by the UPA, later to become the United Press and eventually United Press International (UPI), was the key to its domination of foreign news in the sub-continent for the next three generations.

The lessons of 1914 were not lost on AP. 'The whole point is that we are tied up with three government-owned, possibly government-subsidised, propaganda services. We, a non-profit-making organisation, are tied up with three money-making organisations, and it is an unholy alliance,' complained one AP director, Oswald Garrison Villiard.[2]

There was one man at AP who more than anyone else was outraged by the international news cartel and the way it appeared to work against the interest of his news agency. Kent Cooper was head of the AP traffic department which had received the September cable from *La Nacion*, and he was shocked by the AP's inability to give the customer what he so obviously needed. For Cooper it was the start of a lifelong crusade to convert the other news agencies to the idea that there should be freedom for each agency to operate how and where it wanted.

As Sir Roderick Jones toured the world's capitals, he was treated in a fashion appropriate to one who 'controlled the greatest pool of international news in existence'.[3] At Vancouver, the liner due to carry him across the Pacific was ordered to wait until his trans-continental train from New York arrived. Each of two identical presidential railway coaches was put at his disposal to transport him across China. The former Chinese Prime Minister, W. W. Yen, pointed out to Jones that news despatches from his agency were so respected that the word 'Reuter' had passed into Chinese dialect as a synonym for 'truth'.[4] The Governor's launch met his ship in Hong Kong, and he was the principal guest at Government House there, in Singapore and in Ceylon. In the Indian capital, New Delhi, he naturally stayed at the vice-regal lodge. In Japan the premier prince of Japan hosted a dinner held in his honour attended by the Prime Minister, the Foreign Minister and the most senior government officials.

When he steamed into Yokohama harbour, his was the first ship allowed in after one of the world's most devastating earthquakes which killed nearly 100,000 people. Back in London, the manager of Reuters' commercial services, Cecil Fleetwood May, spotted the cabled news from Japan and rushed copies round to the silk merchants in Wood Street in the City of London. Fleetwood May had grasped that businessmen were prepared to pay high subscriptions for topical news as well as prompt and accurate prices. This was Julius Reuter's old business creed but nevertheless an eternal truth for the news agency. But Jones, basking in the welter of social engagements across the globe, had failed to understand that businessmen and financiers were as hungry for news as the ordinary newspaper reader.

The problem was that a division had grown up within the agency between those on the bridge – the news men – and those in the engine room, the men who were providing the profitable commercial services. The money-making ventures on which Julius and Herbert Reuter had embarked had either disappeared or were on their way out. The advertisement department had gone, apart from a profitable out-station in Australia. The remittance business was fading away, while the telegram business was declining and would close within a few years. Jones had only himself to blame. He noted much later that he 'never cared for these supporting sidelines'.[5] His interests lay in the mainstream of political and general news for newspapers. It was true that he gave limited support to the development of economic news services, the foundation of the original Reuters business, which operated from a garret at the top of the Old Jewry office. But their work was dismissed by the bilingual newsmen downstairs who wrote and rewrote the cabled news on which the reputation of the news agency now depended.

These Reuter employees were Bohemian types, a cosmopolitan bunch who took a pride in being able to compress as much information as possible into the minimum number of words, whether the language was French, German or English. They took the news from Havas and Wolff, in Paris and Berlin, and, together with Reuters' own reports and the contribution from AP, wired the cables to clients across the world.

While the cost per word of each cable sent was gradually falling, it was still the most significant part of the company's expenditure. Compression was therefore the key to profitability and, naturally enough, could lead to occasional misunderstandings. When the Reuters man in New York sent a story in 1901 headed 'McKinley shot buffalo', he was signalling the assassination of the American President at the Great Exhibition in the Niagaran town of that name – not his shooting prowess on the prairie.

Similarly, cables sent from London could be misinterpreted. When Australian papers came up with the story 'the admiral in command of the Turkish fleet has bombarded the port of Dulcigno on the Adriatic Sea', it was an inspired guess. The actual cable from Reuters in London had read simply 'admiral bombardier dulcigno' and gave the result of the big race at Newmarket. The use of cables and the hazards of words mutilated in transmission were to continue for many years. As late as World War Two, during the war in the North African desert, Reuters put out a story which was carried by all the leading Argentine papers and covered the arrival in Suez of the very important General Kennelsone. It was some time before it was noticed that the despatch in fact was a general summary of the situation in the Suez Canal Zone. The ingenious editors in Buenos Aires kept the general alive for several days, during which time he made a tour of inspection, before he was 'killed off' in a plane crash.

When Jones took over as chief executive the number of correspondents who were paid as full-time employees was very small. For the main part, all the news agencies employed 'agents' who were paid small sums for the news sent and subsequently used. Stories were usually copied from locally published papers; the idea of original reporting or of obtaining stories at the same time or before local newspapers was the exception. However, the reputation of Reuters was already such that to be a recognised Reuters correspondent was in itself an honour. It opened all sorts of doors and provided the sort of contacts of which Roderick Jones had taken full advantage.

So long as Reuters news reports retained their quality and reliability, the agency, with its ready-made international cable network, appeared invincible. But subscribers had begun to object that the news was too official and too British. The Australians, for example, complained regularly that the choice of the news service they received should be made in Reuters' London offices by Australian and not by English journalists. When Jones raised the subscription rates to both newspapers and agencies, the chorus of complaints grew. He was accused of failing to provide the brighter, faster stories of competitors. The tell-tale sign of decline appeared when the British United Press, an offshoot of the American United Press Associations, drove a wedge into Reuters' jealously guarded newspaper market in the United Kingdom.

For a while, it looked as if Reuters might be able to keep the competition at bay. The new agreement on the international news cartel, signed just three days before the Armistice which ended the First World War, had not been unfavourable to the British agency. But, significantly, the new treaty allowed the AP to distribute its service within Latin America in competition with Havas and United Press. Within five months, AP was serving twenty-five newspapers.

The American challenge, led by Kent Cooper at the AP, grew by the year. The AP often lambasted Reuters for being the propaganda organ of the British Government. To the untutored eye, Reuters appeared fair game. Jones himself, after all, had assumed responsibility for directing British Government propaganda during the First World War. His avowed interest, and that of the British Government, was, first, in news from the Empire. News from the rest of the world took second place. But some of the AP's criticism was wide of the mark. The stigma attached to an international news agency for being to some degree both nationalistic and partisan was not as great as might be imagined. Indeed, it was expected, just as the support of each national government for its national news agency was a matter of course. For all their bluster, the Americans were no different from their British rivals. The AP considered it had a moral duty to trumpet the successes of the United States. When, for instance, the founder of the United Press Associations, Roy Howard, went on a sales mission around South America he took a letter of introduction from President Woodrow Wilson in his pocket.

If news followed the cable, so too did commerce. American businessmen soon noticed, for example, that it was no coincidence that South Americans and Europeans considered the United States to be a dangerous country, overrun with hostile Red Indians, whose exports were shoddy and whose cars were liable to melt in the tropical heat. They blamed this ignorance on the lack of an American news presence.[6] Properly exploited, they argued, an American news service could be used to the advantage of big business, boosting its image and promoting its successes.

The US Government, too, was uneasy about the international news cartel which shut out its agencies from areas deemed to be of national interest. It objected strongly to the fact that the main American territorial possession in the Far East, the Philippines, was receiving American news via Reuters in London; they saw it as being altered and rewritten to produce an anti-American slant. When one of the AP directors, V. S. McClatchy, testified before Congress that such foreign control of news was prejudicial to

American interests, Congress ordered the US Navy to open its trans-Pacific radio circuits to its news agencies at rates low enough to compete with the British.[7]

The Americans saw Reuters' overwhelming strength in cable as the biggest obstacle to their own global ambitions. They also suspected that the British Government was manipulating the cable tariffs to suit Reuters. Their suspicions had some foundation: the British already operated discriminatory cable tariffs in favour of empire news traffic and Jones was heard constantly to complain that it was impossible to set up new services or keep them going without being given a special rate.

But the AP was not above playing the same game, given the chance. When Havas obtained a cut-rate deal of twenty-five American cents a word for sending its news to South America, the private owners of the American cable in New York came under intense pressure from the State Department to offer similar competitive rates to the American agencies. The American cable company agreed and pushed its rate down to sixteen cents a word – for American clients only. The Americans thought this would protect AP against its fast-expanding rival United Press, but also force the French agency Havas to hand over its South American news distribution business to its American partners. The French refused to be bullied: whatever the rates offered by the Americans, they would be matched by the French Government, even if it meant slashing them to zero.[8]

When Jones arrived back in London from his world tour he was convinced that the only way to meet the American challenge was through a united front of the British press behind Reuters. At this stage, it was the mere germ of an idea, though in later years he would claim that the idea of turning Reuters into a national institution owned by the press in the United Kingdom was his alone, and one for which he had worked for many years. The truth is perhaps slightly different.

Jones had a clear distinction in his own mind between ownership of the news agency, and the control and way in which it was run. He envied the power of some 1,400 newspapers in the United States which lay behind the Associated Press, but his autocratic style of management scarcely suited the concept of a genuine news co-operative. At forty-four, he was still ambitious. But he had reached an age when, perhaps, it was wise to consolidate. Just seven years before, his partner, Mark Napier, had died and Jones had bought enough shares out of his estate to give him 60 per cent of the company; he became a trustee for the remainder on behalf of Napier's children. As principal shareholder, the financial benefits were by no means clear. No one, not even the board, could be sure how much money he was syphoning off for himself from the company. What was clear, in the year that Jones went on his world tour, was that official figures showed an all-time low profit of £181. It would pick up the following year to £2,081, but the struggle to make ends meet was becoming progressively harder.

The idea of co-operative ventures was not new to Reuters. Jones himself made much of his own success in forming what is today the South African Press Association (SAPA). In 1908, he was faced with a revolt by a large section of the South African press which wanted to contol and distribute its own foreign news in South Africa. Jones successfully defended Reuters' monopoly; but he conceded the principle of a local co-operative news agency in which the newspapers could all join. In practice, Reuters continued to have seven of the twelve shares in the national agency, while the remaining five were divided between the three main English-language South African newspaper groups. The Dutch-language newspapers were left out. The result was that Reuters retained control of the agency but gained in strength because it could count on the full support of leading newspaper owners tied in with the Reuters venture. The arrangement was not uncommon amongst the European agencies at the time and, no doubt, was the sort of coup Jones had in mind when he first sought financial support from the British press.

In the years after his world tour, Jones increasingly canvassed the idea of selling Reuters to the London and the provincial newspapers. His initial suggestion was that the two groups should take 51 per cent of the shares, split in equal parts so that Jones was left with what amounted to a controlling 49 per cent. The Fleet Street national newspapers, divided as ever, backed out of the deal at the last moment. But the Press Association, which linked the provincial newspapers in a loose grouping for the purpose of sharing the costs of reporting, pressed on with enthusiasm. When the London papers officially withdrew from the proposed venture on November 3, 1925, the provincials were delighted and Jones went to their decisive board meeting to find the directors in a mood of 'schoolboyish gaiety'.[9] The men from the privinces had beaten the rich and powerful barons of Fleet Street to the punch and gained control of what they saw as the most prestigious news agency in the world. Buying Reuters was an insurance policy: it allowed the provincial papers to control their sources of foreign news. But there was an added attraction: the small men were now the prime source of foreign news to their bigger brethren in London.

On December 31, Jones surrendered control of the firm by selling 53 per cent of the Reuters shares to the Press Association. But as the Associated Press and its new general manager, Kent Cooper, cynically observed, the Press Association had taken over Reuters 'in a technical sense but Sir Roderick Jones remains in charge of the orgnisation'. The wily managing director of the British news agency had calculated carefully that the British press was sufficiently divided against itself not to interfere with the way he ran the company. His autocratic style would remain unchallenged. He had, as Kent Cooper wryly noted, 'eaten his cake and kept it'.[10]

The new PA representatives left the management to an individual they trusted, just as they left the handling of their own domestic network in the autocratic hands of the Robbins family, father and son, for fifty-eight years. They had no desire to run Reuters themselves nor to delve too deeply into an international news organisation about which they knew nothing. Besides, Jones was careful to keep them ignorant.

Jones was richer by £160,000, he had a ten-year contract, and a commission of 10 per cent of the profits made by the agency. But he was still running an empire under continuous attack by the Americans. Within two years the Associated Press denounced the international news cartel contract and only agreed to a new one on one condition: that the service which it provided would be considered on equal terms with that provided by Reuters. AP now refused to pay a cash sum annually to Reuters to reflect the differential in the quality that each had previously attached to their respective services.

At the same time the board of management of the Associated Press decided to set up plans for a full international operation, with new reporting offices outside the United States providing AP's own news service to customers. In April 1931, Jones watched helplessly as Associated Press started up a limited liability trading company in London. Similar operations were also set up in France, Germany, and the other main international centres.

Was it mere coincidence that at the very time when Reuters was being squeezed harder than ever before by its American rivals, Jones all but sold out his shareholding in the company? Under the 1925 agreement, the PA had an option to buy all but 1,000 shares in the agency and it exercised that option in 1930. Jones picked up £157,000, enough to maintain his expensive lifestyle. It was a very good deal for the man who had preferred to remain anonymous during the 1916 rescue: despite the company's poor profits record, Jones had managed to sell the bulk of his shares to the PA for a sum approaching £320,000, a king's ransom in those days.

With hindsight, Jones' financial withdrawal appears prophetic. AP's rapid expansion continued apace and, by 1933, its foreign reporting costs at around half a million dollars were equal to, and maybe exceeded, those of Reuters. That year came the final straw, in the same country where Jones had been extravagantly entertained and fêted just ten years before: Japan.

Until 1914, virtually all the news that went into or came out of Japan was controlled by Reuters. That year the British agency encouraged a group of local businessmen to set up a national agency, Kokusai. By 1926 this had turned into a newspaper co-operative with the name of Rengo and its new title in English, Associated Press of Japan, reflected its affinity with the American AP and interest in securing the best possible service of North American news. Kent Cooper saw the chance to break another Reuter stranglehold and pressed his advantage. In 1933, without telling Jones, he signed a contract with Rengo (later to change its name to Domei) that gave Associated Press equal status with Reuters in Japan.

Jones was livid and immediately retaliated by cancelling Reuters' 'news swap' contract with AP. His co-directors and owners of the firm were horrified. In one rush of blood, chairman Jones had cut Reuters' news report from one of its most important sources, North America. They ordered Jones across the Atlantic to negotiate a new agreement.

Kent Cooper at the AP was blunt. For years he had waged war against 'Reuters Rex', fulminated against its domination of the world news market, and complained that his own AP news service was filtered and rewritten by men in London determined to use it to damage American interests throughout the world. Today his claims look exaggerated and preposterous. But when Jones sat across the table in negotiations, they were deadly serious. After hours of talks, the Americans forced Jones to concede the right to AP to distrubute its news services anywhere in the world.

As Jones steamed – literally – back to London, he must have been afflicted by some self-doubts. He had steered Reuters through difficult times. He had organised not one, but two rescues in an effort to preserve the agency's independence. But the agency's strength had derived not just from his own tempestuous leadership but most of all from its monopolies granted within the international news cartel. Once that monopoly cracked, there was no possibility that a European news agency could make profits on the sale of news alone or on purely domestic services. Reuters would have to find other sources of finance if it was going to survive.

SECRET SUBSIDIES

'Sir Roderick has throughout been most anxious that this grant-in-aid should not be represented publicly as implying any Government interference with Reuters.'
—Foreign Office minute, January 12, 1938.

Reuters' secret relationship with the British Government began with the arrival, on Sir Roderick Jones' desk, sometime in the spring of 1937, of the company's accounts for the previous financial year. The news was bad, and it looked as though worse was to follow.

The company's net profit for 1936 was £14,076, the lowest for the last ten years, and a 14 per cent drop on the previous low of £16,391 in 1931. The net dividend paid to the Press Association was down by nearly 40 per cent from its peak. At a time when competing news agencies were expanding across the globe at an unprecedented rate, Reuters, the most prestigious of them all, could not afford to keep pace. In the light of the estimated real turnover of £1,500,000, the true nature of the financial problem quickly became apparent. The very survival of Reuters was now in danger.

As the threat of war drew closer, Jones' thoughts turned increasingly to the methods that had helped him rescue the company during the previous world war. At that time Reuters had operated a special world news service sponsored and paid for by the British Government. Only the signature at the end of each message – '*agence reuter*' instead of the usual '*reuter*' – revealed that there was more to this news than met the reader's eye.

During World War One, Jones also ran a Government information department which authorised Reuters to operate a service of some 10,000 words a day (against a payment of £126,000 in 1918). Even Government accountants considered this to be 'open to objection'.[1] As a 50 per cent shareholder in the agency, Jones, in effect, was taking a profit on each word of propaganda transmitted by his own, supposedly independent news agency, a curious twist of responsibilities which had not gone unremarked in Fleet Street circles.

Some two decades later, Jones' aim of reversing the agency's fortunes could once again be interpreted as having a dubious moral purpose. By the autumn of 1937, the Government set up a Cabinet Committee, under the chairmanship of Sir Kingsley Wood, then Minister for Health and later to become a member of Chamberlain's War Cabinet and Chancellor of the Exchequer, to examine the whole question of the overseas broadcasting of British news. It was a golden opportunity for Jones to exploit his high level contacts in government.

Jones could look to powerful connections with the Prime Minister, members of the Cabinet, the Treasury and even Sir Kingsley Wood himself. His object was to use every means available to secure the best possible deal from the Government without having to sacrifice Reuters' much vaunted image as an independent and impartial news agency, uncorrupted by government money. But if the price of securing a subsidy was to be the desecration of these values, and the reorganisation of the company under firmer Government control, then that would be necessary to save Reuters from ruin. His great fear was that the secret relationship should leak to the public or a Reuters' client.

During the summer and early autumn of 1937 Jones set about drafting and tentatively advancing a number of schemes. Initially, they were little more than a development of the World War One model: Reuters would increase the supply of British news abroad, particularly to those countries in Europe, the Colonies and the Dominions and in return receive financial concessions from the British Government.

In the middle of November, Jones went to see the Prime Minister, Neville Chamberlain, and asked if the Post Office could charge a discounted rate for any British organisation that could deliver a special service for wireless transmission to specific clients. Jones did not hide the fact the only agency capable of providing such a service was Reuters.

Chamberlain saw the importance of extending world coverage of British political views at a time of deepening tension in Europe. But he suggested that Jones discuss the matter with the Postmaster-General, Major G. C. Tyron, the Cabinet Minister responsible for the Rugby and Leafield international radio transmitting stations which broadcast the Reuters services.

At a meeting on November 23, Jones presented the Postmaster-General with a memorandum outlining Reuters' request for assistance from the British Government for increasing British propaganda or, as the Foreign Office put it, 'publicity' abroad.

According to the Foreign Office files:

Reuters' position, and with it British interests, are now seriously threatened by the News Agencies of Germany (DNB), France (Havas), Italy (Stephani), and Japan (Domei). These agencies, financed by their governments (Havas to the extent of over £250,000 per annum, and DNB believed to be more) are flooding the world . . . with tens of thousands of words daily not only of their own national news but also of foreign (including British) news at a price with which Reuters, conducted on an ordinary commercial basis, cannot possibly compete.[3]

Jones stressed the undesirable consequences of having British political views and public opinion presented to the world through anti-British news agencies, and suggested that the Government authorise the Post Office to reduce their transmission charges for Reuters. The news agency would transmit 6,000 words a day to Europe and 6,000 words a day to the rest of the world, all for the same price that it was paying for its wireless telegraphic news service to the whole world. Reuters would bear the heavy extra costs of staffing and other expenses of conducting these enlarged services. 'This means nothing more, nothing less, than authorising a special rate,' Jones' memorandum concluded.

It was pointed out to Jones that the service which Reuters transmitted to the Continent consisted of only 1,000 words a day, with the same amount going to the rest of the world. The world service was broadcast from Rugby in ten daily transmissions from Monday to Saturday, with 300 words sent out in two transmissions on Sundays.

Jones' proposal amounted to a request that the Government pay out £50,000 a year underwriting transmission from Leafield and Rugby, some 90 per cent of the cost of the new services.[4] Seen in isolation, the request in 1937 for a 'special rate', which sparked off the whole subsidy issue, appears aggressive and self-seeking. It is however, important to consider what Reuters paid for its communications in the context of world communications costs at that time.

The price of sending information, in whatever form, has been dropping consistently since the beginning of the century. Transatlantic telephone calls made by the general public have fallen by over one hundred times in real terms over the last fifty-eight years (£1.63 a minute in 1983 compared with the equivalent of £173 in 1927).[5] For Reuters with their specialist techniques the reductions have been even more dramatic.

Jones suggested that a special rate could prove beneficial not just to Reuters but also to Cable and Wireless, and a strong case can be made that he was right. The Government gave this publicly quoted company a special concession in 1938 when they cancelled the standing rental for the Rugby transmitter for which Cable and Wireless had paid £250,000 a year. In exchange the Government took 2,600,000 £1 shares in Cable and Wireless. The return in dividends from these shares were never expected to be as much as the rental of the transmitter and the exchange was done in the national interest and 'the great importance on political, commercial and strategic grounds in maintaining intact the company's system of Imperial communications'.[6] The Government lost around £100,000 a year but was able to appoint a director to the Cable and Wireless board. As things turned out, World War Two increased the volume of Cable and Wireless traffic by 400 per cent and in 1940 profits doubled to £2,375,000.

Roderick Jones was not alone in complaining that British communication costs were too high. The European manager for the United Press, Webb Miller, pointed out in a letter to Sir Robert Vansittart, the Chief Diplomatic Adviser at the Foreign Office, in October 1938, that the American agency used Dutch transmitters for much of their world service because they were so much cheaper than the British. His views were all the more convincing because, as Miller pointed out, the Dutch had no propaganda aim. 'They were all doing it solely for the money there is in it, and they find it possible to make money.'[7]

Where Jones differed from everyone, including the Americans and the British Foreign Office, was that he wanted the reductions for Reuters alone. The British Government already operated discriminatory cable tariffs in favour of Empire traffic and Marconi – which preceded Cable and Wireless – had operated a press tariff since 1907, and an Imperial press rate since 1909. The American agencies felt these special rates gave Reuters an unfair edge and had been complaining formally since 1929.[8]

At the meeting with the Postmaster-General, Jones pushed his claim for a special rate by insisting Reuters would incur extra costs to provide this vital propaganda service for the Government. The meeting ended with the Postmaster-General suggesting that Jones' proposals be taken up discreetly with the Foreign Office. What the Reuters chairman's gentlemanly discussion did not reveal was that this scheme raised larger questions about public funds being voted to a private enterprise, particularly one which was involved in disseminating independent news.

Five weeks later, on December 28, 1937, and following a Cabinet decision, the Secretary of the Kingsley Wood Committee issued the following ('top secret') amendment to the committee's terms of reference:[9]

> To consider what steps should be taken to improve, enlarge and facilitate the distribution of news from this country, whether by wireless telegraph or cable, with particular reference to the position of Reuters and their application to the GPO for special facilities.[10]

In other words, the Government was sanctioning an official inquiry into the possibility of a disguised subsidy to Reuters in exchange for Reuters increasing the distribution of British 'news' abroad.

Jones' pressure had paid off, but he was far from home and dry. The professionals at the Foreign Office were opposed to the idea of a subsidy – whether open or secret. The Foreign Office specialist on Reuters was Rex Leeper who some four years previously had conceived the idea of the British Council. Leeper was not taken in by Jones' charm. He wrote to his Whitehall colleagues that Jones' demands amounted:

> to a request for a handsome disguised subsidy as a result of which Reuters would be in a favoured position not only in relation to foreign competitors but also in relation to British competitors within the Empire and more particularly the Dominions. It would only be a question of time before the latter were driven out of business.

The effect of such a subsidy would be to alienate the other Empire press agencies, with the risk of damaging British 'publicity' abroad. The same argument applied to Reuters' erstwhile American partners whose claims that Reuters was a government-subsidised agency would become stronger and more credible.

The Foreign Office mistrusted the real motives behind Jones' application for a Government subsidy. One Foreign Office minute suggested:

> They have now decided to take full advantage of the present sympathetic atmosphere, and possibly to exploit Foreign Office anxieties about the news situation abroad generally, by laying claim to assistance on a much wider front. . . . If a disguised subsidy on such lines were contemplated a much tighter form of control would be necessary to ensure not only that the content of the messages was satisfactory, but that the charges made for the services to subscribers abroad would be fair. Otherwise Reuters might be in a position to hold to ransom their poorer foreign and colonial clients and the purpose of the subsidy – wider dissemination abroad of news from Britain – would be defeated.[11]

On January 4, 1938, the Kingsley Wood Committee held its fourth meeting to consider the new Reuters proposal.[12] Its members agreed that Reuters was fighting a losing battle against highly subsidised foreign competition and against powerful American agencies backed by a large and extremely wealthy newspaper clientele. So much was straightforward.

The Treasury representative, Sir Alan Barlow, then raised the tricky question as to how the subsidy was to be paid. Would the cost of running the new Reuters transmissions at a loss be borne entirely by the Post Office, which presumably would give the concessionary rates? If not, the losses would have to be borne by the taxpayer by charging them against the fixed contributions to the Post Office from the Exchequer. This second alternative would require statutory authority. Concealing the subsidy would be impossible unless the Post Office itself was prepared to underwrite the losses. It was a consideration that was to plague the Government – as well as Reuters – throughout the rest of the protracted negotiations.

When Sir Roderick Jones addressed the committee he made out his case largely upon the lines of his memorandum submitted earlier. But this time he made particular reference to the situation in South America.

Jones began with an explanation of how much of the world was carved up into news zones between Reuters and the French agency Havas. In 1927, the two agencies amended the anti-competition agreement, and Reuters ventured into the South American market. The attempt was a failure and, according to Jones, the losses largely explained the company's poor financial position in the mid-thirties, by which time Reuters had pulled out of South America.

The Reuters chief said the South American market was swamped by poor quality news from foreign agency sources. Although the better Latin American newspapers appreciated that Reuters provided 'a more reliable, sober and dispassionate (and) high(er) class of news', they simply could not afford to pay for it at unsubsidised rates.

Jones said he was arguing his case on 'high policy': the enhancement of British prestige abroad. It would be bad, he said, for British prestige if Reuters went down – not, of course, that there was any prospect of this. He told the committee he was also arguing on business grounds. The Post Office would benefit from the increased traffic. Indeed, he continued with enthusiasm, the proposal was so good a business proposition that he did not regard it as a subsidy – either direct or indirect – at all.

But by focusing on South America, Jones had left himself vulnerable.

Sir Kingsley Wood ordered the Foreign Office to conduct a

detailed survey into foreign news agencies' penetration of the South American newspaper market.[13] The resulting study showed clearly that the wireless news services of Germany and Italy were hardly used at all in the South American papers. Of twenty-nine daily papers in Buenos Aires, Rio de Janeiro, Santiago and Montevideo, one week's foreign news was broken down into the following news agency sources:

United Press	55.8%
Associated Press	15.6%
Havas	17.8%
Special (including own correspondents)	7.3%
Transocean	2.4%
Other sources	1.2%
	100.1% (sic)

Anti-British propaganda did not appear to be quite the problem claimed by Jones. It was looking as if Jones' plea for a subsidy was more to bolster Reuters' balance sheet than serve British propaganda purposes.

Throughout the spring and summer of 1938 the battle between Jones and the Foreign Office over the proposed subsidy grew fiercer. In a counterblast to the Kingsley Wood Committee on April 13, the Foreign Office argued that 'no subsidy be given to Reuters or preferential telegraphic rates which could be represented as such'.[14] The FO was in favour of a generalised reduction in cable and wireless rates, a closer degree of co-operation between British Official Wireless (the official Government news service), and the provision by Reuters of a news service to the Foreign Office on a commercial basis.

The main aim of the proposed initiatives, the Foreign Office insisted, had to be to help Reuters maintain its reputation for impartiality and, as far as possible, to improve its services. The idea of an official subsidy was 'foreign to British traditions'.

The Foreign Office brought up its South American guns: 'It is to be feared that in consequence of the . . . disingenuous arguments of Sir Roderick Jones many of (the committee's) members may have been left with a false impression' as to the real difficulties in South America, and as to the actual need and contingent practicability of a genuine penetration into that market. It was vital that good relations be maintained with the North American agencies, and, anyway, no conceivable amount of financial help could possibly do Reuters any good in this direction.[15]

The Foreign Office noted also that the British Chambers of Commerce in South America, worried about the effect of declining British publicity on their Latin American markets, had written to the Prime Minister asking for an open subsidy to be given to Reuter. Indeed, Reuters were not the only British company that sought to exploit the Government's growing interest in subsidising a British news service. The Exchange Telegraph Company through one of their senior managers, H. P. Smolka, wrote to Sir Robert Vansittart and suggested that the Government should give a £16,000 to £20,000 annual subsidy to his company 'for a news service (for propaganda purposes) from this country to the continent'.[15]

The FO, however, had drawn its own conclusions about Jones' special pleadings: what was needed to effect 'those little amendments in Reuters' practice, which the experience of the FO suggests are desirable is the elimination of certain leading personalities in the present Reuters'.[16]

Jones, oblivious to the Foreign Office plans, concentrated on out-manoeuvring the threat which such rival solicitations might pose to his Grand Scheme. Through what appears to have been a systematic and deftly executed exploitation of his high level contacts, he spent the remainder of the year, and a good part of 1939, lobbying in an attempt to anticipate, if not to pre-empt, the formal proceedings of the Committee on Overseas Broadcasting.

The evidence that Jones' private lobbying was aimed at bypassing the Kingsley Wood Committee was substantial enough to have made the Foreign Office complain about him. Indeed the matter was so sensitive that only a select few at the Foreign Office and Treasury were kept informed. On the Reuters side, one of the three general managers certainly knew exactly what was going on, and perhaps two of them. But the Foreign Office was most anxious that the third, Christopher Chancellor, should be kept in the dark. Chancellor had been brought back to London that year after running the company's affairs in the Far East, and Leeper at the Foreign Office had plans for him:

> The whole question of relations with Reuters is at present the subject of negotiations with which other members of the department are unfamiliar. These negotiations are of a most confidential nature and the fact that they are proceeding should not be passed on to Mr Chancellor.[17]

On his side, Jones was keeping his board of directors informed on the points that he wanted them to know of the negotiations, but he carefully concealed mention of the subsidy and the other conditions that were going to be attached to the Government money. At the regular board meeting the general managers were allowed to sit and listen to the discussion. They were not allowed, however, under any circumstances, to speak.

Chancellor had at this time already stated explicitly that he was firmly opposed to any Government subsidy, though he was, somewhat naively, in favour of some form of assistance to help the company keep its business in Japan, China and Hong Kong. His frustration at the board meeting grew as he listened to Jones relate what he suspected to be a tissue of lies.

By the end of April 1938 Jones had won over Sir Kingsley Wood to his point of view, as Leeper observed to Sir Alan Barlow, the Treasury Under Secretary:[18]

> It is the Minister's view that what we should now look for is a scheme or schemes prepared by Reuters for ensuring the reception and publication of a full and improved news service in certain 'key' countries and a statement of the approximate cost that would be involved in each case.

The 'key' countries involved were to be Portugal, Spain, Yugoslavia, Greece, Rumania, Turkey, Egypt, China and Siam (Thailand). The Foreign Office was furious. Having won half the Whitehall battle Jones went all out to break Treasury resistance.

On Thursday, July 7, 1938, Jones had his chauffeur drive him from the Reuter offices at Carmelite Street to Whitehall. There he held a private meeting with Sir Horace Wilson, the personal adviser to the Prime Minister, Neville Chamberlain. At this meeting, the last of several between the two, the final wording of the secret contract was thrashed out.

The Foreign Office file, containing the only publicly available copy of the document, is marked *Reorganisation and Subsidisation of Reuters Limited*.[19] It shatters the idea of Reuters' image as an impartial and independent news agency, untainted by Government money or political interference. Not surprisingly, the file was only recently declassified and made available for public inspection.

The document is accompanied by a covering letter from Wilson to Jones, dated July 11, 1938:[20]

> In accordance with the promise I made to you on Thursday last, I send you herewith a note embodying what I turst (sic) you will agree are the main points upon which we have agreed in our recent

conversations. I have not thought it necessary to include in this document the general understanding which you and I have reached as to the relationship between H.M. Government and Reuters; these are sufficiently on record already. Nor have I, of course, attempted to include in it personal assurances which you have given me as to your own desire to co-operate as we would wish.

. . . the financial arrangements will in any case require further discussion with the Treasury.

We share your view as to the advantage of being able to take early action on the lines agreed; I hope, therefore, that you will be able to do what you suggested on Thursday, namely place the matter before your Board within the next few days.

The document, headed *Reuters* and marked 'secret and confidential', is divided into three sections and is worth quoting in full.

1. It is understood that Messrs Reuters intend to make certain changes in their organisation, viz:-

    (a) The abolition of the combined office Chairman and Managing Director.

    (b) The appointment of Sir Roderick Jones as Governor and Chairman, and of X as Chief General Manager (X to be a younger man and acceptable to H.M. Government no less than to the Board) who shall be responsible to the Board. The question of acceptability would be reviewable throughout the initial period of five years, the intention being to ensure that X is capable not merely of fulfilling adequately the position of Chief General Manager, but of developing in such a way as would justify his appointment to the more responsible post at the end of five years.

    (c) The immediate delegation of certain of Sir Roderick Jones' powers to X so that (1) he shall have the active daily management of the organisation, including staff, and become fitted to take full control, and (2) Sir Roderick Jones shall be liberated at once to engage in the larger development of Reuters in the interests of the state.

    (d) That at the end of five years, sooner if Sir Roderick Jones so wishes or later if the Board and he so agree, while retaining the position of Governor he devotes only half his time to Reuters. Subject to further consideration at the time the Chief General Manager would become Managing Director; the question whether he also became Chairman would be considered at the time by the Governor and the Board.

(e) That at the end of a further five years, sooner if Sir Roderick
Jones so wishes or later if the Board and he so agree, he
retires from active daily work in Reuters but retains the
position of Governor.

(f) That Sir Roderick Jones' tenure of office under b, c, d, and e
be subject to the stipulation that if he be totally incapacitated
and unfit for one year to perform his duties he shall at the
discretion of the Board surrender his position and retire completely from Reuters.

The financial and other arrangements attaching b, c, d, e
and f will be a matter of arrangement between Sir Roderick
Jones and the Board (Sir Roderick Jones has given Sir
Horace Wilson certain explanations about this).

2. When these changes have been agreed, the Government will
make a payment to Reuters for the purpose of assisting them to
extend and improve their foreign news service, i.e. not only the
collection of news but in particular its dissemination overseas,
with the object of providing the Government and the public
overseas with an accurate and impartial service of news,
especially on topics or events in which British interests are concerned.

3. The Payment will be made on the following conditions:-

(a) Reuters will at all times maintain the closest co-operation and
liaison with the Foreign Office and other Government Departments at home and through their agents overseas. While
maintaining complete independence of direction and control
by H.M. Government they will at all times bear in mind
suggestions made to them on behalf of the Government as to
the development or orientation of their news service or as to
the topics and events which from time to time may require
particular attention.

(b) H.M. Government will review at the end of 1939 and at
intervals thereafter the progress made by Messrs Reuter in
achieving the objects indicated above, and the continuance
of the payment will depend upon the Government being
satisfied with the progress achieved.

(c) If Messrs Reuter's net proftis in any year including the
payment of H.M. Government, exceed their average net
profits for the years 1934, 1935, and 1936, the payment (for
that year) will be reduced by a sum equal to 60 per cent of the
excess. Messrs Reuter will supply the Foreign Office with
copies of their annual balance sheet as presented to their
shareholders and with such financial statements of income
and expenditure as they may require, and will allow a representative of the Foreign Office, if the Foreign Office desire it,
access in confidence to their books of account. (N.B. It will

be necessary to have agreement as to the basis on which profits are to be calculated.)

(d) The payments will be based on the net estimates of costs incurred or to be incurred by Messrs Reuter in improving their news service to and from countries specified by or agreed with the Foreign Office. To begin with it is contemplated that the payments should cover the following arrangements as they come into operation:

Increased news service in certain European and other countries £665 p.m. (say)	£ 8,000
Extension to the rest of Europe	1,000
South American Service	17,000
Salary of Chief General Manager (say)	3,500
Increased payment to G.P.O.	10,000
	£39,500 p.a.

(e) Messrs. Reuters will supply their news service free of charge to the Foreign Office and to certain other Government Departments and to British Missions and H.M. Government's official representatives overseas as requested by the Foreign Office.

3. Provision for the payment will be made in the Vote for Diplomatic and Consular Services.

These secret Foreign Office minutes constitute the 'Gentlemen's Agreement' between Jones and the British Government. From this moment, a black one in the agency's history, the Government became intimately involved with the affairs of Reuters, even to the point of having a say in the appointment of the next Chief General Manager. The Foreign Office had no intention of letting Roderick Jones stay on as Chairman of Reuters for longer than was absolutely necessary. The Mr X, the new Chief General Manager, was to be groomed as Jones' successor, if possible with Jones' agreement. For the supposedly independent Reuters board, unaware of this 'Gentlemen's Agreement', the implications were devastating.

For the Government, the 'Gentlemen's Agreement' presented numerous difficulties. How was the subsidy to the concealed from the public and Parliament? Jones insisted that the appearance of impartiality and independence, so crucial to the news agency's prestige abroad, had to be preserved. And yet such subterfuge and deceit ran the risk of Ministers misleading or even lying to Parliament.

The Government had decided against deceiving Parliament by

disguising the subsidy, but the question of the Government's paying the salary of the Chief General Manager (now to be called the Joint General Manager) would give rise to questions 'which might be difficult to answer'.

By September, however, the approaching war in Europe was beginning to influence the Government's thinking on the matter. Hitler's tanks had rolled into the Sudetenland, and Czechoslovakia was about to be sacrificed to Chamberlain's policy of appeasing the German dictator.

Sensing how the international crisis could be exploited, Jones hurried over to No. 10 Downing Street on the very morning of the day that Chamberlain went to Godesberg to meet Adolf Hitler.[21] The quick confirmatory note to Wilson and Barlow explained that 'during the present emergency, it would be a good thing if Reuters disseminated in South America the extra 2,000 words which . . . it was agreed that they should eventually do when the scheme for subsidising Reuters went through'.[22] The note went on:

> The first section of the service will be started during tonight, and we hope to have it well developed over a large part of the Continent and the Far East within the next twenty-four hours. Additional territories will follow as quickly as possible.

Jones was overjoyed. His own comment on the Downing Street meeting was ecstatic: 'the permission I sought was immediately given! Thus was achieved in five minutes what red tape had blocked for nearly ten months. By teatime the first enlarged series of Reuter wireless news despatches was beamed and broadcast to the agency's distribution network everywhere. In less than a week stimulating evidence of the galvanising effect of the service was reaching us from all parts of the globe.'[23]

The extra cost of the newly extended services from the Leafield and Rugby transmitting stations was some £10,500 for 720,000 words a year at three-and-a-half (old) pence a word. Reuters agreed after consultation with the Treasury that an invoice for the extra transmission costs was to be sent to the Foreign Office every month, vouched for by a copy of the account which they had received from the Post Office. For the next few months Reuters transmitted a government-subsidised service amounting to an extra 2,000 words a day from each of the Leafield and Rugby stations. The money was to come from the Diplomatic and Consular vote, and the Foreign Office was warned that it would have to defend it.

The extent to which the Government was prepared to hide the

subsidy became clear when Godfrey Nicholson MP presented a written question in the House of Commons to ask the Postmaster-General whether, amongst other things, the Reuters extended news service received preferential rates; and whether they received any financial contribution from the Government. The Postmaster-General's reply was:

> The charges for their transmissions are computed on a commercial basis, having regard to the volume of traffic and the conditions of the service; and the same principle would be applied to fixing the charges for the news messages of any other agency.

The House of Commons appeared, on the whole, to be sympathetic to the idea that Reuters should get special treatment. At any rate Jones drew considerable comfort from a debate earlier in the year when, on February 16, 1938, one speaker asserted that the best means of counteracting foreign propaganda was 'by the widespread dissemination of straightforward information and news'. Jones was particularly impressed by the fact that the House carried, without a division, a motion which urged the Government *to give the full weight of its moral and financial support* to the wider and more effective presentation of British news, views and culture abroad' (Jones' italics).[24]

Throughout the autumn of 1938 Jones was helped by key Reuters executives in working out ways by which the Government could be persuaded of the efficacy of a disguised subsidy. William Turner, one of the three general managers, wrote to a Mr Bowyer at the Colonial Office suggesting ways of 'camouflaging the amount of emission charges' so that they did not appear more than those charged by the British Post Ofice to such competitors as British Official Wireless for a similar service. But discrimination against foreign news services in British colonies 'would be a matter of high policy which would require the sanction of the Cabinet'.

Nevertheless, by February of the following year, Sir Kingsley Wood was preparing to go over the heads of the Foreign Office representatives on his own committee to try and persuade the Foreign Secretary, Lord Halifax, to ignore the advice of civil servants and support a grant-in-aid. Leeper wrote to Halifax on February 13:[25]

> I gather that Sir Kingsley Wood does not accept our objections, but wishes to discuss the question with you personally.
>
> I presume that his main argument will be that Reuters are the only agency we have for the dissemination of our point of view and that

we must therefore attempt to improve them. It is proposed to do this by giving them a grant of £25,000 and making certain alterations in their central organisations, which will make it more efficient.

In the FO we do not believe that these proposals will achieve the aim desired. We feel that Reuters have no chance of competing with the heavily subsidised and controlled foreign agencies unless they are equally subsidised. This would involve a very large sum from public funds. We believe that the £25,000 proposed will achieve no appreciable results and that it will in fact be a pure waste of money.

Our alternative proposal is not to subsidise Reuters at all but to make a general reduction in press rates in this country in order that all agencies, foreign as well as British, and Dominions, may send more news from here. That will be financially welcome and useful, whereas a subsidy to Reuters alone will arouse criticism. The subsidy will fall on the FO vote and the FO would have to meet the criticism. The FO which in every desirable direction have taken the lead in urging expenditure on propaganda are opposing this expenditure because they do not believe it will really serve our propaganda.

While Kingsley Wood was lobbying the Foreign Secretary, Jones himself had written another memorandum outlining the Reuters case and submitted it in person to Sir John Simon, the Chancellor of the Exchequer.[26] The memo, dated January 4, entitled 'HMG and Reuters' was also submitted shortly after to Halifax and it stressed that there was no question of the agency making a profit out of the subsidy. It also reminded Sir John of the deal struck up at a moment's notice as Hitler prepared to strike at Poland:

During the crisis in September Reuters enlarged their wireless service on the Government's account and the enlargement is still being maintained; but this is only a provisional arrangement and is in any case a half-measure compared with the balanced and comprehensive plan which has been under the consideration of Sir Horace Wilson, Sir Alan Barlow and Sir Roderick Jones ever since last spring. It is most desirable that the position be regularised and British publicity abroad be strengthened without delay, as is now proposed. Precious time is being lost, during which foreign subsidised agencies are steadily entrenching themselves.

As Jones' campaign intensified, the Foreign Office, galvanised by the thought of having to defend the proposal in the Commons, brought its full intellectual weight to bear on the matter:[27]

The proposal under consideration is the grant of an open subsidy to Reuters of £25,000 per annum. If this is approved it will probably be attacked on political grounds as representing a departure from the traditional principle of Government detachment in regard to news services. Reuters' position would be entirely changed. Except in regard to two important factors they would then be in the same position vis-a-vis the Government as are their chief continental competitors DNB and Havas.

These factors are:

(1) Unlike the German and French Governments, His Majesty's Government would not have control of the content of the Reuter messages while they could hardly escape responsibility.

(2) The suggested subsidy being so much smaller than that of their French and German rivals, Reuters, while losing their prestige of independence, would not gain the advantage of a fuller and better service. From this it would follow that, if the principle of a subsidy is accepted, it would have to be very much larger to be effective. That would certainly necessitate some control by HMG. It might also lead to heavier subsidies by other governments to their agencies. That control, however, Reuters will not accept.

The Foreign Office memorandum goes on to point out that Reuters' most formidable competitor in foreign (that is to say non-Colonial and non-Dominion) countries was probably the United Press of America, and that to enhance the extent of Reuters' coverage in areas already covered by United Press would be likely to encourage the American agency to discredit Reuters as no longer being an independent agency. The memorandum then goes on to raise the effect of Dominion agencies:

More important politically are the probable effects within the Empire of a subsidy to Reuters. Thus strengthened financially, Reuters would, almost certainly, attempt to recover ground lost to the Dominion agencies operating from London. The latter have at considerable expense rid themselves of Reuters' tutelage and would keenly resent the re-entry of Reuters into their market if it were made possible by assistance from HMG (His Majesty's Government).

It was not merely the lack of substance in the Reuters case for a subsidy which the Foreign Office raised in its submissions to the Foreign Secretary. The style with which the lobbying was conducted caused more than a few official eyebrows to be raised. Leeper had noted indignantly on January 9:[28]

Sir Roderick Jones' message to the Secretary of State constitutes an attempt to override an inquiry into the whole question of British news services abroad which has been proceeding since a Cabinet Committee was set up under the chairmanship of Sir Kingsley Wood twelve months ago.

Just three days later, on January 12, he was even more personal in his minute to Lord Halifax:

Sir Roderick has throughout been most anxious that this grant-in-aid should not be represented publicly as implying any Government interference with Reuters. The Foreign Office have informed the Treasury that they are not prepared to advise their Secretary of State that this grant should appear on the FO vote and that an FO Minister would have to defend it.

I am informed, however, by the Treasury that Sir Roderick has succeeded in capturing the fancy of Sir Kingsley Wood and that the latter would have preferred an even larger grant to Reuters and is not at present willing to accept the Foreign Office view that no grant should be made. I may add privately – though this is very private – that the Treasury officials at heart sympathise with our point of view.[29]

Therein lay the power of Jones' high-level Government connections. He was able, albeit after a long battle, not only to override an official Cabinet Committee studying the Reuters proposal, but also to overcome the persuasive and highly influential arguments of the top Foreign Office and Treasury civil servants. Like the subsidy proposal itself, this testified to the lengths to which Jones was prepared to go in order to save his company, a campaign which included the subversion of the traditional mechanism of government itself. But the civil servants had their own friends. And Jones had enemies within his own camp. It would not be long before these combined forces drove him from office.

6

A QUESTION OF TRUST

'I cherished the delusion that Reuters' independence was no mere myth.'
—McLean Ewing, deputy chairman of Reuters, 1941.

In the spring of 1939 they began removing the scaffolding from the top of the most imposing building yet erected in Fleet Street. Designed by one of the leading architects of his day, Sir Edwin Lutyens, it was to be the culmination of all the dreams of Sir Roderick Jones, the headquarters of the world's most prestigious news agency and the news capital for its junior brethren throughout the Empire. Jones would have thought it only fitting that his new building was to be built on the site where his country's greatest diarist, Samuel Pepys, had been born.

But Jones' vision of greatness had lost touch with reality. The bulk of the money for the new building had come from the agency's owners, the Press Association. Jones was indignant that 'his' company was being treated as a 'mere tenant'. The Fleet Street barons were expected to be autocratic, and their lifestyle sensational: Jones considered he was due no less. On his arrival at the office each morning bells would ring in every room and passage, and it was only when similar bells rang in the evening to announce his departure that staff could relax. The timing had to be impeccable. At the precise moment when he left his office a messenger boy would be alerted and start jumping up and down on the rubber strip in the road in front of the traffic lights. The lights would turn to green just as Jones' chauffeur pulled away from the kerb. As an employer Jones was not popular, perhaps because of his insistence on the 'strictest observance of infinitesimal minutiae'. One young man who started work as the third and junior secretary to Jones left no doubt about his personal dislike of Jones – and found it reciprocated. James Lees-Milne, who later went on to the National Trust, noted that Jones' face 'resembled that of a wasp seen under a microscope. It was long and the bulbous nose was proboscis-like. His small eyes darted rapidly in his head in the manner of that insect. They never rested on their victim, yet because of a feverish activity missing nothing. His mouth too was sharp and vespine. His sting was formidable and unlike the bee's could be repeated.'[1]

His attention to detail covered both his activity in the office and his entertaining. Flowers would be despatched personally and presented to a departing lady at the railway station or dockside. Waiters would stand behind each guest at splendid dinners organised at his London home in Hyde Park Gate where he lived with his wife, the well-known novelist and socialite, Enid Bagnold. Younger than her husband by twelve years, she married Roderick not because she was in love with him nor for his money but, as she admitted later, because he made her do so. She had 'no choice' in the matter: Roderick Jones was 'an irrevocable man and what he wanted went'. She bore his vanity: 'Not of his achievements, not of his brains. Of his slight figure. He loved to look at his outline in full length in the glass.'[2] There were few neighbours who could keep up with the Joneses. Apart from his personal emoluments and income, his 1931 contract with the company allowed him an expense allowance of £2,500 a year for which he did not have to account.

It was clear that Jones preferred the company of the well-known and well-bred to some of the owners of provincial newspapers who sat on his board and had no title and little experience of the world. When he sold the company to the Press Association in 1925, the new directors had been content to leave the management of the news agency in his hands. They had participated in the discussions, uncertain as to whether the London newspaeprs would join in or not. Having won through, they left Jones to carry on unchanged and unchecked.

The rotation of directors meant that an entirely new set of men, unfamiliar with the circumstances of the 1925 rescue, now sat around the boardroom table. They were no longer content with the lack of information about the company's affairs. As the years wore on, they increasingly resented Jones' tactless and cavalier treatment.

By September 1939, the relationship between Sir Roderick Jones and the board had deteriorated sufficiently for McLean Ewing of the *Glasgow Herold*, deputy chairman of Reuters, to write a private and confidential memorandum to the five other Press Association directors. Ewing had been chairman of the PA in 1935–1936 and he was going to be chairman again in 1941–1942. He was critical of the amount that the PA had originally paid for Reuters and the way in which Jones had built up his company's balance sheet by valuing its holding in subsidiary news agencies outside the United Kingdom at between ten and twelve times their annual profits. When some of these agencies eventually bought their assets and goodwill from Reuters at one-third of Jones' valuation, Ewing noted dryly that 'Sir Roderick's estimate must have been regarded by them as more in the nature of a freedom fine than a purchase of an admitted goodwill asset'.[3] The return of, on average, £18,000 a year on the PA investment of £313,000 had been, in Ewing's eyes, 'not brilliant'.

Ewing was also critical of the amount of money that Jones himself was taking out of the company and pointed up the board's lack of control: 'All members of the board have now got copies of Sir Roderick's contract, and are equally wise or ignorant as to what he has taken out of it in any or all of the last fourteen years. I doubt if any director has ever had the temerity to ask what his "commission" amounted to. . . .'[4]

Even Ewing could not conceal a hint of admiration when he referred to Jones' personal contract which stipulated a salary of £5,500 a year, to be paid 'free of tax'. Jones had explained during the negotiations that 'he was not a grabber and did not want to haggle about the matter'. He was quite ready to drop a demand that his salary should also be paid free of super tax.

Although Ewing and his co-directors were largely kept in the dark as to Reuters' true financial affairs, they were bracing themselves for bad news. Ewing noted in his memorandum that 'the monthly statements are much worse than any I have known', and he predicted the position would deteriorate. The burden of rent and rates for Reuters' new Fleet Street headquarters, occupied by the agency since July, would almost certainly send the trading balance into the red. Ewing went on:

> On top of this we have a state of war which may not bring profit to either Reuters or the Press. We have been assured that economies are being effected in the administration but nothing short of a complete reorganisation of outlook on the part of the Managing Director will save the company, let alone the credit of the Board.[5]

The memorandum, written in the first week of September 1939, was timed to reach the other board members in advance of a special meeting called urgently by Jones for the following Tuesday. The directors had not been told the reasons for the meeting, but Ewing had an inkling that it concerned the agency's relationship with the British Government. 'I fear greatly that it relates to a subject regarding which his (Jones') sanguine expectations have been disappointed,' he noted.

The board meeting, held on September 12, did not prove to be the disaster that Ewing had feared. Jones tabled the draft of a contract with the Government which, in its essentials, was the same as the one that had already been running for the past year. There was, however, no mention of the 'Gentlemen's Agreement' on the Government subsidy, nor Wilson's covering letter to Jones which had established the 'general understanding' between Reuters and the Government since July 1938. The contract presented by Jones excluded South America and the rest of the western hemisphere from the expanded transmissions for which the Government was paying over £18,000 a year. This figure was made up by a payment of £7,500 to cover editorial and other expenses, £3,000 as a subscription to the Rugby transmission service, and £7,000 as payment to cover the additional Post Office charges for the Leafield transmission to Europe.[6]

In practice, these figures were expanding considerably, so that by July 1941 the Government was paying 50 per cent more for the Rugby service, and all the costs of the Leafield transmission. However, Reuters credited to the Government any subscriptions they managed to collect from war-torn Europe. The Government, in addition, paid for all transmission costs to Latin America in 1941 and guaranteed any trading deficits that might be incurred there; it paid for a special service transmitted from India to Hong Kong and Singapore; it picked up the costs of translation into French in London; it paid for certain reception equipment, inward cables from key Commonwealth capitals and it helped substantially with correspondents' costs in Ankara, Bangkok, Hsinking and the Balkans.[7]

On the face of it, the board meeting on September 12 was a triumph for Jones. Ewing congratulated his chairman on two years of tough negotiations with the Government and the board minutes note his comment that 'it was clear that there was no question of a subsidy; the proposed Government payment would be simply a payment for news services to be supplied'. Jones was even able to tell the board that he had arranged that Reuters' name should not appear in the public accounts. The payment would be included in the Government funds allocated to 'Foreign Publicity'.

Despite the board's retroactive approval for the contract there were two directors present who had strong reservations. One was William Haley, newly joined that year as a director from the Manchester *Evening News* and shortly to leave to become Editor-in-Chief of the BBC and then its Director-General; the other was Samuel Storey, Member of Parliament for Sunderland and chairman of the Portsmouth and Sunderland newspapers group. It was Haley who spotted the maggot in the apple: the wording of the contract which implied, in his view, some measure of Government conrol.

Jones was loath to reveal the full extent of his secret dealings with the Government. By revealing as little as possible, he hoped the board would eventually come round. In private correspondence between the Secretary of State and himself, he conceded that the contract might be worded differently. But, again, he blandly insisted that there was nothing, either verbal or in writing, between the Government and himself that detracted in any way from the absolute independence and impartiality of the news agency. Otherwise, he insisted, he would never have been party to it himself, nor asked the board to endorse it.

In retrospect, one has to wonder how much Haley knew when, towards the end of the meeting, he asked chairman Jones for an assurance that any attempt by the Foreign Office to influence Reuters in a manner contrary to Reuters' traditions would at once be reported to the board.

Over a year had gone by since the gentlemen's agreement had spelled out the contract which provided for Government financial assistance once the requisite changes in Reuters' organisation had been made. The civil servants understood Jones might have problems persuading his board. Jones had, in fact, already suffered one setback when he introduced Christopher Chancellor at a board meeting as a new general manager without any previous reference to his fellow directors.

It was precisely the row over Chancellor's appointment which triggered Ewing's September 1939 memorandum. Ewing was empowered by his colleagues to talk to Jones and to insist that changes be made in the company's organisation, including the provision of more information about the company's activities and consultation about senior appointments. It appeared to Ewing that Jones might be trying to foist Chancellor on the board as his successor. Jones assured him that nothing was further from his mind.

By January 1940 it was clear that the board were tiring of Jones' arrogance. His contract meant that the earliest date the board could get rid of him was the end of the following year and, as the war in Europe turned against the Allies and France fell to the German invasion, it did not seem wise to change the top management at short notice. But there were also rumbles from within the company and Ewing was invited by three senior executives to have a talk about their boss. The three unnamed individuals insisted that the way in which Jones was running the company was becoming increasingly dangerous.[8] Advice offered was not taken, and any hint of criticism of the headstrong man who had dominated the agency's affairs for more than twenty years was impossible.

During the long hot summer, as British and German fighter aircraft fought the Battle of Britain over the Kent coast, discussions between Jones and James Henderson, then chairman of the Press Association, took place as to the timing and detail of Jones' departure. By November 11, Henderson confirmed formally to Jones that he would leave at the end of December 1941 and receive a pension of £5,000 a year. But even at this moment, a crushing one for his pride, Jones failed to disclose to the Press Association directors his secret agreement with the British Government.

When Churchill succeeded Chamberlain as Prime Minister, he quickly turned his attention to the Ministry of Information and ordered the department to assume full responsibility for propaganda. He left the director general, Sir Frank Pick, in no doubt that propaganda was to become a key weapon in the future conduct of the war. Pick already knew that Churchill distrusted the BBC and its 'pontifical mugwumpery', and he even warned his opposite number, the director general, F. J. Ogilvie, that the Government might well take over the BBC. The Press Association itself was under pressure from Government censorship, and the Ministry's own news division was emerging more openly as an offical Government news agency.[9] In these extraordinary conditions, it was perhaps only natural that the Ministry should take over responsibility from the Foreign Office for negotiating Reuters' contract.

At the first of several meetings, Pick produced a draft document entitled 'Heads of Agreement between the Ministry of Information and Reuters'.[10] This document went much further than the contract which had worried Haley and Storey. By December 5, after two more meetings, Pick presented the board with another draft for which Jones wanted to secure quick and formal agreement. But the directors were nervous. James Henderson noticed that the copy circulated by William Haley differed in key respects from the copy in Jones' possession. If Haley's copy were the correct one it would 'reduce Reuters to a condition of slavery' and no new agreements could be made by Reuters without Government consent. One clause, in his opinion, made Reuters merely a vehicle for circulating Government 'dope' and gave any British Government in office up to the end of the war the right to issue 'comment, guidance or interpretation on *any* item of Reuter news. How is the British press going to react to this? . . . the clause still stinks in my nostrils'. Haley attacked the way in which Reuters was expected to heed the Government's 'advice' upon the appointment of individual correspondents overseas. However, on the whole, Haley accepted that the final draft was not at all bad.[11] Even as they debated the agreement Pick resigned and was replaced by Sir Walter Monckton as director general at the Ministry of Information.

In retrospect, the issues seem simple. The Govenment needed the fullest possible backing from the press both in Britain and all over the world for the war effort. Faced with military disasters on every side and the prospect of a German invasion at any moment, it was vital to use every means available to keep up morale. The Government wanted to control both the Press Association and Reuters.[12] The PA was not so much a problem because the rules of censorship could be easily enforced at home. But Reuters supposedly controlled itself; the Government was powerless to interfere in much of the news that it despatched abroad and even less in the news gathered overseas and transmitted to Britain for home consumption. Sir Roderick Jones had been an asset in World War One. Now he was a liability.

The directors of Reuters, who were all provincial newspapermen and directors of the Press Association, also wanted Jones out, but for different reasons. They were no longer content to be mere puppets like the directors under Julius and Herbert Reuter. Had the financial position of the company been sound they might have taken a different line. Their concern was that Jones was leading the company into deeper and deeper financial trouble. Jones usually managed around the month of May to produce a rabbit out of his hat and save the company's profits but increasingly the directors were sceptical.[13] These were not the men who had negotiated with Jones and bought his company from him. They had not bought Jones' sense of 'vision'. They did not know what was really going on and they mistrusted him.

Jones himself worked on the patriotism of the PA directors and the need to go along with Government wishes in the name of the national war effort. But his own position was more complicated. His contract authorised him 'to act in such manner as shall be in the best interests of the company'.[14] He revelled in his vice-regal position, with his powerful social and business contacts and his total domination of those who worked for him. Blind megalomania prevented him from seeing that his secret dealing would eventually be discovered and bring him down.

It was William Haley, later described by staff on *The Times* when he was editor as being the only man with two glass eyes, who finally saw through Jones. In his first few months as a director of Reuters, Haley had come to know and make friends with Christopher Chancellor. He stayed frequently with Chancellor and his wife at their flat behind St Paul's when he came down to London from Manchester for the Reuters board meetings.[15] Both Haley and Chancellor were members of the four-man team from Reuters who met Sir Walter Monckton at the Ministry of Information on January 20, 1941, to discuss the proposed new agreement. Samuel Storey was due to attend but pulled out. The other Reuters men were William Moloney and Jones himself.

There are two accounts of that meeting.[16] One was prepared by the secretary to the committee, a Ministry employee, the other, marked 'private and confidential', by someone on the Reuters side. It was Haley who, in the Reuters version, emphasised that 'Reuters must not only remain independent but also have the appearance of independence'. It was Haley who, again in the Reuters version, argued that Reuters should not 'consult' the Government on the appointment of any successor to Jones. 'The Government would be advised beforehand, but would not be consulted,' he said. To this 'Sir Walter nodded'.

The Ministry account, referring to what might happen if the present chairman and managing director ceased to occupy that post, noted the director general as saying 'it was possible that this contingency might not long be deferred'. In the Ministry version, it was 'both Sir Roderick Jones and Mr Haley (who) emphasised the importance they attached to there being no document in existence which, if made public, would convey the impression that Reuters were under Government control'.[17]

Monckton then made reference to a letter from the Foreign Office Minister Lord Perth to Sir Roderick Jones in September 1939, mentioning a 'new draft agreement' between the Government and Reuters. The penny apparently failed to drop. At a second meeting, on the Friday of the same week, with Storey present, Monckton asked Haley and Storey bluntly if they were aware of all the correspondence related to the 1939 agreement. Had they not seen the letter dated August 24 from Lord Perth at the Foreign Office to Jones and which formed an integral part of the agreement? Haley and Storey were dumbfounded. At the critical September 12, 1939 board meeting, Haley had specifically asked Jones for an assurance that any attempt by the Foreign Office to influence Reuters would be reported to the board. The assurance had been given. Yet now it appeared Jones had all along

been in possession of proof of exactly such Government influence.[18]

The two PA directors turned to Jones and demanded the letter.
Jones stoutly denied its existence and said that the agreement
stood by itself and there were no other letters that had any bearing
on it.

Haley was not satisfied. On Monday, February 3, he reported
back to the PA members of the board at a special meeting in
Leeds. The meeting continued the following day in the train down
to London on the way to the main Reuters board meeting. Jones
was to have been briefed in advance by Ewing in the gentlemen's
lavatory but fate that day dictated that the lavatory was closed.
Jones went into the boardroom unbriefed and accompanied by his
own lawyer. He sat down in silence. There was an open window
behind him and Jones indicated he could feel a draught. One of
the members got up, shut the window and sat down again. The
room remained absolutely silent.[19]

At last Jones spoke: 'Does any gentleman around this table
consider that I have deliberately withheld documents from the
board?' There was a short pause and Haley placed on the table two
letters and pushed them across to the chairman.

Haley said: 'I do.'

Jones glanced at them and bolted from the room.[20]

Ewing was deputed to follow Jones across the hall and arrange
for his resignation. The resulting document, dated the same day,
indicates that Sir Roderick Jones 'retired' from Reuters.

Jones' downfall was caused, therefore, by two letters. The first
was the Wilson correspondence, though the second – the so-called
'Perth letter' – has achieved greater notoriety. It added little to
Wilson's except for the short handwritten postscript which,
perhaps more than anything, was repugnant to the owners of
Reuters. It read:

> P.S. Since the above letter was drafted I learn that you propose to
> appoint Mr Christopher Chancellor to the post referred to in Para-
> graph A above. I have pleasure in informing you that Mr
> Chancellor's appointment to the post will be acceptable to His
> Majesty's Government.[21]

Paragraph A of the agreement entailed a new post of 'Joint General Manager' acting as direct deputy to Jones. The individual
would be in charge of all the arrangements in the 1939 agreement
and within eighteen months he would be named 'Chief General
Manager'. The post of chairman and managing director would be

reviewed within five years. In short, the British Government had assumed responsibility for sanctioning the appointment of the agency's two top managers.

Jones' departure did nothing to resolve the embarrassment of the secret relationship with the Government. Samuel Storey was appointed unpaid chairman by the board and the day-to-day running of the news agency fell to the three general managers, two of whom were in London. Two of the three were nearing retirement and, by July 1944, the Foreign Office at last got its way and Chancellor took sole charge.

For the moment, though, the directors were left with a valid and enforceable contract they hated and from which they could not escape. It would be difficult to repudiate an agreement given that Jones could argue a good legal defence that he had been 'acting in the best interests of the company'. Ewing was despondent: 'Until Monday, 3rd February, 1941, I cherished the delusion that Reuters' independence was no mere myth,' he wrote.[22] The only course open was to co-operate to the fullest extent with the Government and hope they might be persuaded 'to ignore, if not to tear up, the humiliating and objectionable document'.[23]

The trouble was that Jones' grand scheme was paying off. Ewing noted 'Reuter has been receiving great publicity on the wireless and observation leads me to the conclusion that the Reuter service has enabled the Government to get over essential propaganda . . .'. As a result Ewing felt confident enough not to press for a complete return to the old conditions: 'A sound defence against criticism lies in the plea of national necessity in wartime.'[24]

There was, however, a longer term problem. Ewing was not alone in his worries about the need to reorganise Reuters. There was a fear that the London newspaper proprietors might become restive under an arrangement which compelled them to purchase not only home but foreign news from an organisation where they lacked any representation.

The Newspaper Proprietors' Association had missed its chance in 1925 to buy into Reuters due to its own internal bickering. Fifteen years on, the London newspapers had a bigger circulation in the provinces and a greater appreciation of the value of provincial news. If pushed hard enough, it was possible the NPA might extend the nucleus of its own home news gathering organisation and become a strong competitor to the PA. In addition, the London newspapers had considerably more foreign correspondents, while the American agencies and London's own Exchange Telegraph were only too keen to extend their own operations in Britain.

The departure of Jones made London newspapers even more interested in how the news agency was to be run. Individual proprietors telephoned Jones in his office immediately when they saw the announcement of his resignation on the ticker tape. But the deal struck with Jones precluded any explanation and he begged them to make no comment in their papers.[25]

Ewing and some of the other directors felt now was the time to suggest to the London newspapers that they take some sort of stake in Reuters. At this stage, in late February, three possible schemes were proposed.[26] The NPA might appoint one or more directors to the board of Reuters even though they had no shareholding in the company; the NPA might become part owners in Reuters; or there was the possibility that Reuters might be turned into some form of national trust. The board decided to make some preliminary soundings.

Haley's contacts led Chancellor to Lord Rothermere, proprietor of the *Daily Mail*. Chancellor's own contacts – his wife is descended from Lord Gladstone – took him to Lord Camrose and to Lord Layton, who controlled the *News Chronicle*.[27] Within a month, urged on by Lord Rothermere, the London press barons made a formal approach to the PA and indicated they wanted to join the Press Association as joint and equal owners of Reuters.

But it was not to be that simple. The German bombing of London was at its height. St Paul's cathedral burned and outside the front door of the Reuter and Press Association headquarters a 1,250 kilogramme land mine was caught suspended in the trolley bus lines. After the building had been evacuated for three-and-a-half hours the mine luckily came down upside down and was rendered harmless.[28] Inside, the old animosities and suspicions between the London and provincial press owners were proving less easy to defuse.

The provincial press were principally concerned that the sale of half the Reuters shares to the NPA would change the balance of power between the two. The London papers would not only hold half the Reuters shares. Through their provincial editions and provincial papers allied to them, they would continue to hold a 25 per cent interest in the Press Association, and through the PA, in the PA half share in Reuters. However, the London papers were themselves divided, with Lord Beaverbrook of the *Express* switching between a firm partisan to an outright opponent of the scheme, as he saw his arch rival Rothermere taking a lead in the negotiations.

The weeks drained away and the haggling showed no sign of producing any agreement. At the end of July, Churchill appointed his own man, Brendan Bracken, as Minister of Information. His task was to turn the Ministry into a powerful war-winning instrument. Bracken's predecessors were largely to blame for the low reputation of the Ministry: the 'inept' Lord Macmillan, the 'frustrated' John Reith and the 'urbane, indecisive' Duff Cooper.[29] The new man moved in with reforming ardour, backed fully by Churchill whom he had supported, almost alone, when he was on the backbenches. Bracken took over Wilson's room at 10 Downing Street, occupying the same unobtrusive but powerful position as Parliamentary Private Secretary to Churchill that the civil servant Wilson had assumed with Chamberlain. Bracken was a realist and cynic. He was also a successful journalist who had bought the *Financial News* and *Investors Chronicle* in 1928 and was later to merge the *Financial News* with the *Financial Times* in 1945. A confidant of Beaverbrook, he enjoyed the false rumours that he was Churchill's bastard son. He knew and admired Haley and it was he who eased Haley into the BBC as Editor-in-Chief two years later. Above all, Bracken could not resist intrigue. Precisely this combination of qualities enabled him to bring the individual press barons to heel into one, almost unanimous unit and agree to the terms laid down by the Press Association.

It was Haley, however, who revived the original idea of turning Reuters into a trust. As one of the three PA negotiators in the talks, he put the idea to the press lords at their next meeting.[30]

This time the London press owners were sceptical. 'What does the NPA gain from the Trust?' asked Lord Kemsley, owner of *The Scotsman* and *The Sunday Times*. Haley's answer was that it would build Reuters into incomparably the greatest news agency in the world, completely independent, and deliver steadily expanding and improved services at much reduced fees. The draft preamble to the Trust was typed out by Haley in Chancellor's seventh floor office at Reuters.[31]

The management of Reuters itself had reservations. A report by the joint general managers said it was 'theoretically sound' to expand the ownership to include the press of the whole country. It was one of the facts of life that Reuters enjoyed pre-eminence abroad but did not have the same reputation at home, particularly in London papers. If the NPA's decision to join in ownership meant they recognised Reuters as a national asset, then the general managers approved. But they scoffed at the idea that it would produce lower subscriptions for the British press. They pointed out that Reuters' revenue from India alone was greater than everything it received from the British newspapers. 'Newspapers abroad are being disproportionately taxed to provide a service cheaply for the British newspapers.'[32]

The report of the general managers was written before Haley

presented his Trust idea to the press lords. The problem was that the Reuters board itself was now split. Samuel Storey, chairman, supported by James Henderson from Belfast, were totally opposed to what they considered to be a sell-out to the London interests.

Furthermore, the board of the Press Association, the company that owned Reuters, had decided to recommend the sale of half of its share-holding to the NPA. But a revolt, led by the *Yorkshire Post*, demanded an emergency general meeting to debate and decide the question among the full membership. The rebels said that if the directors with business associations with some of the NPA members had originally abstained, a majority of the PA board would never have voted for the sale. The majority of the PA consultative committee – the 'wise men' – many of whom were ex-PA or ex-Reuters directors, were also against the sale.

Various drafts of the objections circulated among the PA rebels. One put his finger on a key weakness in the scheme. The idea of a Trust had persuaded many PA members they would be safe from control by the London papers. But as one draft pointed out: 'the Trust is camouflage only. The Trustees will have no real power. They will not hold the shares or the income arising therefrom, and while they will appoint the Directors of Reuters, they will only be able to appoint persons nominated by the Shareholders.'[33]

At the time this crucial weakness in the Trust appeared not to matter. Forty years on, as the PA and the press lords were to discover, the flaw was to have a decisive influence on events.

On October 17, as sixty-six members of the Press Association filed into the conference room overlooking the burned-out shell of St Bride's Church, the tension was obvious. Many members, good friends the previous year, were now not on speaking terms. Ewing, as chairman of the PA, justified the sale of half the Reuters shares on the grounds that it would make for a stronger British news agency; it would improve the value of their existing investment and lastly, and of marginal importance, it would prove of financial advantage to the PA.[34] The opposition was fierce.

Led by Samuel Storey, speakers attacked the threats and pressure put on PA members. They accused the London press lords of tactics ranging from plain 'unfriendly' to 'somewhat domineering' and even 'contemptuous' of the Press Association. They considered the editorial standards of the London newspapers to be low and questioned whether their offers of co-operation would be matched by past experience of 'rivalry, cut-throat competition, and their downing of the other man'. Storey even compared them with the limerick about the lady of Riga who went for a ride on a tiger. 'Three men from the Reuter-PA boards went out for a ride with two press lords; they came back from the ride, Reuter-PA inside, and a smile on the face of the press lords.' As for the proposed Trust with its high-sounding phrases, Storey considered no man with any self-respect could hold office. Other speakers called it 'a very curious arrangement' and asked whether anyone with any sense would settle his own money in that way. The main complaint was that 'the Trustees do not have a Trust'.

Malcolm Graham of the Wolverhampton *Express and Star* voiced the opinion of many provincial owners who were against the sale because it meant domination of Reuters by London. He and others had been in the middle of the pitched battle between Lord Kemsley and the 'World' series of papers started by Lord Rothermere in several provincial towns. It was a pretty basic issue. If Rothermere was against the provincial evening papers, then Graham and his colleagues were against Rothermere. One of the main reasons they had bought Reuters in the first place was to keep London out.

Personal issues were raised. One of the conditions imposed by the NPA in its purchase of half of Reuters was that Storey should step down as chairman. After his spirited oposition to an NPA purchase, the press lords wasted the blood of this ambitious Parliamentarian. Storey, later to become Lord Buckton, himelf preferred to draw a veil over this and the treatment he had received from the majority of his colleagues.

Ewing told the meeting that the deal had been agreed and there was a moral obligation to go through with it. The NPA was paying £168,000 for its half-share, the same price it had cost the PA, but he did remind those present that the PA had always regarded its purchase 'as more of a trust than an investment' – words that were to be tossed back at the owners of Reuters time and again over forty years later.

As the votes were counted it was clear outside pressure had been applied in the right places. The *Yorkshire Post*, whose representative had been discussing tactics to destroy the sale just twenty-four hours before the meeting, switched support following the instructions of his chairman.[35] In the end the sale was approved by a majority of over two to one, enough to make it clear that the sale was approved by a majority of provincial papers even if the votes of those papers with London ownership or control were eliminated.

Five days later, Parliament debated the issue of the sale of Reuters. Brendan Bracken, as Minister of Information, was the key Government speaker and he made it clear his department had been involved: 'The Chancellor of the Exchequer and I are actually negotiating with the parties concerned.' Nobody raised the issue of just what the Chancellor, the keeper of the nation's coffers, was contributing to such talks. Sir Stanley Reed quoted Sam Weller that it needed 'a pair of double million glass microscopes to penetrate the jungle of finance'.

Since none of Bracken's documents is among the papers released by the Public Record Office, and Bracken himself gave instructions that all his personal papers were to be burned within twenty-four hours of his death, it is difficult to gauge his position. But he must have been aware of the secret agreements with Sir Roderick Jones. He recognised the arguments and the dilemma of the Foreign Office very clearly when he asked himself during the debate whether a Bill to nationalise Reuters would be helpful to Reuters.

'Certainly not,' he answered. 'If a news agency were regarded throughout the world as being the property of the British Government, its news value would be very small.' He recognised that Reuters needed help. Compared with the American agencies, over the last ten to twelve years it had 'lost ground'. What worried Bracken was that this was no Canterbury Cathedral that had to be saved but a highly competitive commercial business. He went so far as to admit that the Government was keeping 'a fatherly eye on something they do not own, and they are still keeping a fatherly eye on the matter'.

How far had the Government been setting the pace in the negotiations for the sale to the London papers? Was it just the threat of competition by the NPA which forced the Press Association to sell, as some claimed? Or did Bracken see this moment as the opportunity to strengthen a national news agency that could in the long run provide real competition for the Americans? The Government was certainly involved in negotiations with the London press lords. Although the deal had to all intents and purposes gone through and the money for the shares been paid up, Bracken was drawn into what was for his Ministry of Information a pressing problem. He felt 'the wisest course to follow is to see how the Chancellor and I fare when we deal with these great barons of Fleet Street'.

A fortnight later, on October 29, the marriage of the Press Association and the London papers as equal partners was formally announced. The formation of the Reuters Trust was presented as the proof of the independence of the British news agency.

Just a few days before, on October 23, Reuters had picked up a transmission from the German official news agency, Deutsche Nachrichtenbüro. In its 6 p.m. broadcast from Berlin, DNB quoted the newspaper *Deutsche Allgemeine Zeitung* which had discussed the Reuters debate in the House of Commons. The German propaganda service suggested 'the debate revealed the moral abyss of the British news service, particularly by the remarks of the British Minister of Information who wishes to sell the ownership in order to deceive the British and foreign subscribers of Reuters as to the value of the news'. For once, German war propaganda may not have been so wide of the mark when DNB commented: 'The question, however, is who is cheating whom?'[36]

THE PRIVATE BENEFACTOR

'We wax indignant when attempts are made to twist the news. To us this is a sin against our craft.'
—Sir Christopher Chancellor, April 1959.

On January 28, 1946, Christopher Chancellor proudly described the 'new' Reuters to the Overseas Writers at a formal gathering in Washington. He had crossed the Atlantic to negotiate a new contract for distributing news with Kent Cooper, the head of Reuters' American rival, the Associated Press.

It was Cooper, the apostle of truth in news, who had lambasted Reuters for being in the British Government's pocket, and Chancellor, anxious to re-establish the agency's reputation for independence, was well aware that he was confronting a somewhat sceptical audience. His speech to the American press was triggered in part by a small but potentially explosive booklet issued by the State Department on the subject of the post-war international information programme of the United States.[1] For the most part the booklet considered how the American propaganda machine could best be converted into a peacetime publicity unit, but in a section devoted to Reuters, it hinted that the British news agency coloured and conditioned its news service in line with British Government wishes. Most worrying for Reuters' chief executive, the booklet quoted official correspondence to back its claim.

In the light of what he knew of Reuters' secret relationship with the Government during the war, Chancellor chose his words with care during his address. He did not say Reuters had never received a government subsidy: he said it had never been subsidised by the British Government in the sense that the French, German or Italian agencies were subsidised by their governments. And he made it clear that the new board of directors were now totally opposed to the idea of Government financial assistance: 'In 1941 the board of Reuters, at a fearful juncture in the history of the war and in the face of misunderstanding and strong pressure, had the courage to say to the British Government that it would be better for Reuters to disappear from the face of the earth than for Reuters to receive any form of favoured treatment or subsidy. All such arrangements were cancelled.'²

In reality, Reuters was not so distant from the British Government as Chancellor claimed. Despite the existence of the Trust, a copy of which Chancellor used to carry in his pocket as tangible proof of the agency's new-found independence and security, Reuters was still in a precarious financial position. The strengthened ownership of Reuters made no immediate difference to the acute cash shortage which had brought the agency to its knees in 1941. Furthermore, Chancellor's speech failed to touch on a number of commercial ventures in wartime which showed how close its relationship with the British Government really was, for all the grandiose language of the Trust document.

One such Government-inspired propaganda project was the Reuter Imperial News Service which continued *after* the Trust had been set up. The service began following a request by the Ministry of Information's Empire Department to use Reuters' channels to increase the flow of Empire news to and from the Diminions. Chancellor, by then one of the general managers, replied on December 4, 1940, that Reuters would charge the BBC and newspapers in the UK a commercial rate of three-and-a-half pence a word for the 2,000 words a month proposed by the British Government.³

Very soon the service began to run into difficulties. A confidential report from the BBC's Overseas News Editor, A. E. Barker, complained about poor quality. By September 1941, the service was supposed to expand to 8,000 words a month, but the BBC judged its own reports from sources such as the Australian War Commission were 'greatly superior to the material received from Reuters'.⁴

Suspicions were aroused and an internal Ministry investigation began into the precise scope of the new Reuters service. The results were highly embarrassing: instead of supplying the extra 8,000 words, the Imperial service only cabled some 3,653 words service from Australia, Canada, New Zealand, and South Africa for the month of May 1941. In June, the figure slumped to 2,586 words.

The fact is that Reuters' connection with the Government's wartime propaganda machine continued well after the 1941 rescue by the London press, a rescue portrayed as the only alternative to Reuters becoming Government-owned. Indeed, on the day that Parliament debated the future of the agency, a Mr Waddell of the Ministry's Finance Department wrote to a colleague: '. . . we are not satisfied about the quality of the material collected but I think it would be sound policy to maintain and attempt to improve it. . . .'⁵

Two weeks after the Trust had been established, Waddell wrote to Chancellor, confirming the extension of the Imperial news service. 'In extending the authority, the Treasury expressed some doubts on the need for subsidising such cables, the cost of which they considered should be borne by Reuters. On the point of quantity, I have myself noticed that during the first three months of the arrangement considerably less than half the authorised wordage was cabled by Reuters, and I feel that unless there is some improvement in both the quality and the quantity we shall have some difficulties in justifying continuation of the arrangement after December.'[6]

The agency's links with the British Government were formalised under a Whitehall committee, the Joint Standing Committee of the Ministry of Information and Reuters. Chancellor, as general manager, sat on this committee. When the tricky question of how to deal with enemy communiqués came up, Reuters produced a paper in 1941 entitled 'Some proposed methods of combating the effect of enemy communiqués other than by suppression'. The line suggested by Reuters was to distribute the enemy communiqués and to discredit them with a blanket Government campaign that would include ridicule, songs, articles, researched facts and even sermons on truth. Reuters proposed that 'whatever corner the enemy communiqués penetrate the Ministry of Information should also subtly go, carrying on through others a persistent spoken, written, broadcast and whispering campaign designed to undermine all confidence in the enemy communiqué system as a whole'. Reuters was convinced it could assist materially in this purpose. The plan was 'to release certain of our counter-propaganda against the communiqués at the same moment as certain communiqués which the Ministry regard as obnoxious. Its inclusion in the same Reuters transmission, other news service, or home or foreign broadcast should seem purely coincidental.'[7]

To vilify Reuters for agreeing to its use as a Government propaganda outlet during wartime is misplaced. After all, these were extraordinary times, and Reuters had little choice but to contribute to the paramount aim of defeating Hitler. With its huge news distribution network, it was, along with the BBC, a vital link in the propaganda effort. The criticism must surely lie in the post-war hypocrisy of those who refused to admit how close the wartime ties, both financial and political, were between the agency and the Government.

It is impossible to calculate how much money Reuters received from the British Government during World War Two since the relevant files in the Government Public Record Office have either been deliberately destroyed, 'lost', 'retained by the department', or are closed until 1990. But it is clear that Government money was flowing into the Reuters coffers as far back as 1940. One brief note from an official in the Ministry of Information's Finance Department refers to 'the present annual rate of expenditure on propaganda through the press': the first item on the list is Reuters; opposite appears the figure £64,000. Apart from the BBC, which received £4,500,000, Reuters is by far the largest recipient of Government financial aid for the first year of the war up to August 1940.[8]

In the aftermath of the war, the ambitions of Chancellor and his board were to restore Reuters to 'its rightful place' as the greatest news agency in the world. The Trust was constant proof that Reuters was independent, and Chancellor was able to travel the world to show off a document which was in fact a brilliant piece of public relations. He was invited by the Greeks and even the Spaniards under the dictator Franco to provide blueprints for their collectively owned national agencies that could operate without government control or subsidy. Other European countries like Italy and France lionised Chancellor and awarded him medals: King Haakon VII Liberty Cross, Officer Order of Orange Nassau, Commander Royal Order of Daneborg, Officer of the Legion of Honour, Commander Order of Civil Merit (Spain), Cross of Commander of the Phoenix, Commander of the Order of Vasa, Commander of the Order of Merit (Italy). However, on scrutiny of the fine print in the Trust, they usually had to admit that its strictures were not for them.

Behind his cool air of confidence, Chancellor knew that the agency's financial position was as precarious as ever. The virtual closure of the world markets outside the United States and Latin America had all but paralysed Reuters' commercial services. The Far East which had contributed profits of £60,000 a year, now produced nothing. Though India and South Africa were making money Reuters was largely thrown back on the resources of its owners, the provincial and London newspapers, and the Government.

The directors were adamant they could not countenance any form of direct Government subsidy nor say in the agency's affairs. But matters were not so simple. Before the end of the war, Chancellor had negotiated a new agreement with Cyril Radcliffe who, in 1941, succeeded Sir Walter Monckton as director general of the Ministry of Information. The three-year deal took effect from January 1, 1945, and entailed the Government paying Reuters on a 'services rendered' formula. The pay-out amounted to £18,000 a year, but it was supplemented by a flexible sum which arrived via the Foreign Office 'in return for use of the service in special ways'. The total itself was not that large; but given the tiny amount of financial leeway in Reuters' finances, it was highly significant. The Government connection, after all, was not so easily dropped.

On the face of it, the Radcliffe-Chancellor agreement was an exercise in mutual backscratching. It was useful additional income for the agency and it allowed Government offices outside the United Kingdom to use the Reuters service and to distribute it where this did not conflict with the agency's own arrangements. The problem was that it created numerous critics within Government missions all over the world, each pressing for their own particular news requirements to be satisfied. What had been intended as a way to help Reuters finance the quality of its news services rebounded, in a volley of adverse comments about the service, compared to its main competitors. The criticism was not entirely unfounded.

By the time the Radcliffe-Chancellor agreement came to be renewed, the responsibility had passed from the now defunct Ministry of Information to a new Central Office of Information (COI). A secret memo in 1948 by James Wardrop of the COI was scathing about Reuters.[9] 'Reports from HM Missions abroad show that Reuters News Agency has suffered a decline in many parts of the world.' Wardrop assembled the critical reports from overseas under five main categories:

(a) That the agency is inadequately represented in a number of countries.
(b) That its management seems to take the view that each one of its foreign posts should be self-supporting instead of making good losses on the swings by profits on the roundabouts, and that in general it appears over cautious in its financial policy.
(c) That it does not attempt sufficiently to cater for the tastes of its customers.
(d) That it does not make use of foreign language services in certain parts of the world where they are in demand.
(e) That its managerial methods are not always sufficiently up to date and that the speed of distribution of its services needs improvement.

The report acknowledged that Reuters would be unlikely to accept the criticisms 'unless they were supported by the considerable body of evidence now in the possession of the Foreign Office and it is to be feared, therefore, that an approach in general terms would have little or no effect unless it were made at the highest level'. And even if Ministers were to make the approach, the COI considered that it might produce 'an unfortunate reaction' as Reuters could well consider formal recommendations from a bunch of bureaucrats as 'unwarrantable interference'. The memo added that 'the available evidence suggests that Reuters' comparative (and it is to be hoped, temporary) eclipse is due in large degree to financial considerations'.

This was the crux of the problem that had occupied so much civil service time over the previous ten years, involved ministerial intervention and Parliamentary debate and finally defeated Roderick Jones. The fact was that Reuters, whether through lack of competition or lack of interest among the British reading public, had never provided an adequate, consistent news service from the Empire. The agency had none of its own correspondents in any member country within the Empire with the exception of India. Reuters' dilemma came down to the price of truth: how to ensure that the agency had enough funds to remain independent of government, or how to ensure that, if the agency was subsidised, this would not compromise its independence. It was an issue which would not be resolved for many years to come. When it was resolved, it fundamentally altered the nature of the agency and let loose the momentous events of 1981–4.

James Wardrop at the COI was well aware of the problem, and he initially took the Government path suggesting that 'it might be advantageous to examine the possibility of giving some pecuniary assistance to the agency, e.g. by increasing HM Government's subscriptions'. However, he covered his tracks by adding: 'Reuters' capacity to sell its news abroad would undoubtedly be damaged by public knowledge of any payments which amounted to a substantial subsidy. It would not be possible to keep such payments secret from other interested parties, and especially from American news agencies, which have so persistently attacked any form of government control of their competitors.'

Having discarded these options, Wardrop concluded the document by suggesting: 'The problem of additional finance would therefore be more satisfactorily solved if it could be found elsewhere than from Government sources'. And so appeared the notion of 'the private benefactor'.

There were two guises in which such a benefactor might appear. In his letter to Sir Felix Pole, chairman of the major British engineering company, Associated Electrical Industries, Christopher Chancellor had suggested that British firms overseas should put pressure on the newspapers where they advertised to ensure they bought and carried Reuters' news service. Chancellor's initiative was largely in response to complaints by firms in markets such as South America that a good British news service would help to sell their products, but they were not getting the right sort of service.

The only alternative was the one suggested by Sir Kingsley Wood when he saw Sir Horace Wilson and Sir Alan Barlow from the Treasury on February 20, 1938. As an internal memorandum in Whitehall shows, it was strikingly similar to COI thinking ten years later:

> He (Wood) had always felt difficulty in openly subsidising Reuters; and that if it was not possible to subsidise them secretly he felt that the proposal for a major subsidy should be dropped. He thought, however, it was worth exploring a smaller payment on lines which could be defended as merely paying for supplying a news service to the Foreign Office and the Missions abroad. For the rest he asked whether it might not be possible to find some benevolent person who was willing to subsidise Reuters for the balance of the sum of £25,000 or £30,000 which was required over a period of, say, five years.[10]

The question of finding a 'private benefactor' was seriously pursued by senior Whitehall officials. On March 23, 1938, Wilson had a private meeting with Jones to discuss the proposal. Wilson revealed that, no matter what the identity of the private benefactor, the same relations between the Government and the news agency which had been understood under the 'Gentlemen's Agreement' of the preceding summer, were to exist once the benefactor had been found. There would be, he said, 'complete co-operation and a desire on Reuters' part to direct their services in whatever direction we thought'.

The benefactor would remain anonymous and Wilson concluded: 'the position would then be that Reuters would regard themselves as under an obligation to Her Majesty's Government for having arranged for the provision of the additional finance'. It followed from this, said Wilson, that the individual concerned would have no say whatsover in the running of the Reuters service. As events turned out it was the Newspaper Proprietors' Association (later renamed the Newspaper Publishers' Association) which came to the rescue at the Government's bidding. But, by 1948, it was clear that the NPA was not the immediate source of cash to finance the improvements in the services that the Government had hoped for and expected. The owners of the newspapers which bought the services of Reuters and which controlled the company still wanted the cheapest service commensurate with quality. They also wanted a service that steadily improved in quality but they were keen to see the fees they paid for the service steadily reduced. It was a hopeless dichotomy of interest and so Chancellor was forced to cut costs still further.

One of the areas he examined was the Middle East where, at that time, there was little obvious scope for Reuters' news or commercial services. So far as the rest of the world was concerned, most of it was a desert full of nomadic tribesmen where a few sheiks were kept under control by a handful of officers from Britain's Colonial Service. The countries themselves were largely artificial creations carved up amongst the Western European nations after World War One. Israel did provide news, and Reuters owned the local news agency there. But the wider discussions about 'The Arab Question' were largely debated in the more comfortable conference halls in Switzerland where Reuters could report cheaply.

Persia had been news of a very personal nature for Reuters. At one point the Reuter family owned it. Almost. In 1871, Baron Julius de Reuter, as he had then become, was granted a concession by the Shah to exploit the kingdom for himself for a period of seventy years. He had the right to build a railway, roads, irrigation works, develop forests, farm the state customs and develop all the mineral and oil rights. The deal was countersigned by the Shah's Ministers. But the rabbi's son from Cassel was defeated by the intrigues and corruption of the wily oriental court. The scheme failed, as those of others had done before him, and he left in 1889, having salvaged the right to found the Imperial Bank of Persia, which went on to flourish as the British Bank of the Middle East.

For the British Government after World War Two, the Middle East was an area of both strategic and commercial concern. It was essential that a British presence survived in an area with expanding oil interests and the Suez Canal through which the oil and the bulk of Britain's trade with the Far East flowed. Since Reuters could not afford the losses involved in trading in the Middle East, the Government moved in. During World War Two it had operated a propaganda service through Britanova, a London-registered company. At the same time, one of Britain's largest magazine publishers, Hulton Press, had started a company called the Arab News Agency (ANA) whose objectives were to operate as press and literary agents and 'to establish news agencies and information bureaux'.

By 1948, when the future of the Radcliffe-Chancellor agreement was due to end, the share capital of ANA had expanded to 10,000 £1 shares and these were transferred to three individuals whose names were to figure in various Near and Far East information companies with interlocking directorships. Maurice Macmillan MP, son of the future Prime Minister, subscribed for 4,500 shares, so did the Hon.

Alan Hare, now returned from his wartime service with the Special Operations Executive to work as a journalist and later to head the *Financial Times* and become a director of Reuters. The other figure was the author and journalist Thomas Clarke.

In the same year that the Hulton share ownership was transferred, a second company was set up called Near and Far East News (Middle East) Ltd., which operated under the name of Nafen. Hare, Macmillan and Clarke were the shareholders, putting in £2,000, £4,000 and £3,998 respectively. The next year Hare and Macmillan subscribed for a further £5,000 shares each and followed this up in 1951 with another £12,500 apiece. Meanwhile, a similar Asian operation was started in 1949 with Hare and Clarke; in 1952 they brought in the journalist and Member of Parliament Woodrow Wyatt with 1,000 shares. This company was called Near and Far East News (Asia) Ltd. There were other companies such as Regional News Service (Middle East) Ltd. and Regional News Service (Latin America) Ltd., International News Rights and Royalties Ltd., and even Arab News Agency (Cairo) Ltd.

The activities of these companies raise an intriguing question: how were they supposed to create a money-making success in areas where Reuters had decided that a news venture was not profitable? Those who were shareholders and those who worked for the company are now vague on that point. For shareholders like Alan Hare, 'it seemed a good idea at the time'. But it was acknowledged that there were political implications.

How these companies were formed, or why and how the shareholders concerned put up money only to lose it, is easy to speculate on but difficult to prove. The point is that at a time when the Government wanted to keep a British news agency presence in the Middle East, and when Reuters had decided not to provide it, a fairy godmother appeared.

Gerald Long, who inherited the Arab News connections when he became Reuters' chief executive, subsequently admitted it was 'an astonishing business'. He acknowledged that, so far as Reuters was concerned, it was 'dangerous' but he sympathised with the predicament that faced Chancellor.

As Long saw it, 'We had a commercial contract with them and what was the choice? You have to cut your coat according to your cloth, and you have to choose your moment when to get out.'

The arrangements made by Reuters with this 'private benefactor' were straightforward. The agency negotiated a bulk contract with Britanova and later with the Arab News Agency, and received a fee in pounds sterling. Britanova and ANA, in return, had the rights to distribute the Reuters service in specified Middle Eastern countries. ANA also provided a report from the Middle East back to London for the exclusive use of Reuters.[11]

So far as Reuters was concerned it was dealing with a bona fide registered news agency under a standard contract. Whatever suspicions there might be as to the exact nature of its agent in the Middle East were best kept quiet.

By the early 'fifties Reuters was transmitting a special service to the Middle East which also included a small amount of material for the commercial services, mainly exchange rates and cotton prices, which ANA also handled. In Cairo, the service was translated into Arabic, transmitted back to London, and relayed out again to the Middle East as the major international Arabic language service for the whole area. By then it was even using modified teleprinters that printed from right to left.

After the Suez débâcle in 1956, ANA was kicked out of Cairo and forced to move to Beirut. By the following year, it had a substantial office there in addition to staff in London, Cairo, Amman, Damascus and other Middle Eastern capitals plus two roving correspondents. The BBC World Service correspondent was based in the ANA offices. Various British newspapers worked out of the Beirut building including the *Observer*, whose correspondent and former Foreign Office mole, Kim Philby, worked there until he fled to the Soviet Union in 1963. While it lasted, the Arab News Agency had a reputation for solid reporting and the manager, Tom Little, was considered in both London and the Middle East as one of the best journalists of his day. He received the OBE shortly before he died.

In 1964, the Arab News Agency ceased trading. It departed as surreptitiously as it had entered the scene just after the war. There is nothing in the accounts of the string of secretive companies to show whether it was a British 'front' organisation for news gathering or just a useful listening post for British Intelligence. All but one of the companies were dissolved between 1973 and 1983, having failed to file annual financial accounts. The exception was World Features Services which ceased trading in 1983 with accumulated losses of £3,846, but net assets, in the form of sundry creditors, of some £16,000. There was only one clue: as soon as Reuters re-established its presence in the Middle East ANA departed as mysteriously as it had arrived. Therein lies a lesson: when Reuters could afford to operate independently, the need for the 'private benefactor' disappeared and with it, the murky and uneasy relations with the British Government.

THE COMMONWEALTH IDEAL

'Let the newspapers of all free nations consider saying to their governments in the name of ultimate freedom and truth – "hands off the news".'

—Sir Christopher Chancellor

A luncheon party in the summer of 1946 in London happened to bring together the influential Australian newspaper proprietor, Keith Murdoch, with Christopher Chancellor and Lord Layton, chairman of the *News Chronicle*. A chance remark by Murdoch suggested, without any real seriousness, that it might be a good idea for the Australian press to buy into Reuters in the same way as the London papers had done during the war years. Chancellor commented from his neutral corner that there was no reason at all to prevent such a deal if that was what all the parties wanted. On April 22 of the following year and with none of the hesitation, pressures and internal squabbling that had characterised the negotiations with the London press barons, the Australian Associated Press formally took up its shareholding in Reuters. On May 12, the New Zealanders followed suit.

For Chancellor this new alignment was the break he desperately needed. The idea of an international co-operative was not new. It had its origins in the 1930s when Norman Smith, the president of the Canadian co-operative news agency, Canadian Press, promoted it at successive meetings of the Imperial Press Conference. For the Canadians, such a union represented a buffer against the American agencies that dominated their own newspapers. Though some interest was shown, no action was taken. At the time, the reason was practical. Two of the strongest agencies in the British Empire, in India and South Africa, were directly controlled by Reuters, and their profits were critical to Roderick Jones' fight for the financial survival of the agency. Despite his aristocratic connections, Chancellor had none of Jones' ideas of personal grandeur: his need was to secure the broadest possible base for Reuters' future.

The idea of a Commonwealth news agency was in tune with the

thinking of the time, with Churchill's call for the unity of the English-speaking peoples and the idea that the dying Empire should be replaced by a Commonwealth. Chancellor owed no allegiance to either the provincial or the national press. It was evident that the London press barons were not going to provide the really strong financial backing hoped for when they joined the partnership. Chancellor was concerned only to build up on an international scale the same sort of co-operative financial base that secured the Americans' Associated Press with its thousand-plus owner-members. The dilemma that Chancellor inherited from Jones had not changed: Reuters needed money to rebuild, compete, and to expand, but somehow to avoid sheltering under the British Government's wing.

The deal with the Australians and New Zealanders secured a firmer base for Reuters to start again in the Far East, one of Reuters' main strongholds, along with India and South Africa, before the Second World War. Reuters' Far East operations, which had extended from Malaya through to Japan, had fallen to the Japanese armies and were being rebuilt only slowly. Until the new alliance of 1947, Australia and New Zealand were not safe markets, despite their British connections and ancestry. Their newspapers had been critical since the days of the first Baron, and the American agencies were continually on the lookout for expansion.

Australian interests had been directed closer to home during the war years and they now wanted an improved news service from what was now South-East Asia, the same area that Chancellor had run for Reuters until 1939. Furthermore, the Australians would pay for more reporting manpower in that part of the world. They would be glad of the prestige, and the costs of sending a Reuters correspondent from Sydney to Singapore were less than a similar individual posted from London.

The following year another opportunity arose: India. After independence, the tide of nationalism was certain to sweep away Reuters' own local agency, the Associated Press of India. The commercial business might survive, but even this was in doubt. There seemed little hope of preserving the financial contributions made by the sub-continent which, it will be remembered, amounted to more than the subscriptions paid by all the London newspapers put together. Reuters sold its agency with 600 employees for £70,000 to a newly constituted co-operative agency, the Press Trust of India. In the spring of 1948, the Press Trust sent a delegation to London to negotiate joining Reuters on the same terms as Australia and New Zealand. By February 1 of the following year, the formal papers were signed.

The deal was provisionally for four years, yet within a month three Reuters directors accompanied Chancellor on a 'goodwill' mission to India to see how it would work out. When they arrived back in London, forecasts were gloomy. The Indians wanted to introduce propaganda into the service and their views on the Trust's explicit demands for independent news reporting were at best lukewarm. There was no possibility that the principles of the Trust would be upheld. 'You couldn't trust them further than you could kick them,' one of the members of the team commented.[1]

Chancellor's dream that Reuters might become a Commonwealth news agency owned by the press of all its member countries was not clouded by his Indian experience. His statement to the Royal Commission on the Press in 1948 was full of optimisim: 'We may be starting a new sort of organisation which cuts across national barriers,' he declared. However, there were increasing signs that the new Commonwealth would not slavishly follow the ideas of the old Empire.

That same year, in South Africa, the Nationalist Party ousted the pro-British United Party. The country was now ruled by bitter opponents of things British, people who commemorated the British concentration camps of the Boer War, had been imprisoned for their support of Hitler during World War Two, and who would eventually take South Africa out of the Commonwealth.

In Canada, the press watched Australia, New Zealand and then India join the Reuters partnership with no desire to join in themselves. The enthusiasm of the 1930s gave way to mistrust and horror as the story of Jones' involvement with the Government trickled through to them. Their unease increased after the American State Department's attack on the British agency for continued Government involvement, despite Chancellor's attempted rebuttal in Washington. The failure to get the Indians to agree to the principles of independent reporting automatically appeared to rule out the possibility that new non-white Commonwealth nations could realistically join the co-operative. The idea that Reuters would be able to sit at the centre of the Commonwealth and profitably control the flow of foreign news as it had done under Jones was probably already out of date. Once the Canadians dropped out, the Commonwealth ideal crumbled.

Chancellor's only alternative was still further retrenchment. Cutting costs meant reducing all commitments. There had been a time when Reuters had expanded throughout the world, setting up their own national news agencies and controlling the domestic news services, as well as providing a market for foreign news under the cartel arrangements. Now the objective was to cut back on every potential liability. The lessons of India and China were stark: internal involvement in such countries could produce splendid profits in the short term; but if the company came to depend on the revenue, the results could be catastrophic if it were suddenly cut off.

Israel was a typical case. Reuters had set up a local agency run by a Mrs Braude and had run it profitably for some time. News from Israel was important to the world service but running the agency posed big problems such as inflation, exchange control, employment and translation which Chancellor neither wanted nor could afford. As Israel struggled for its independence in 1948, Mrs Braude suggested that the agency move from Jerusalem to the new capital of Tel Aviv. The British army, which held the ring between the Jews and the Arabs, felt this was suicide as they were confident the Jews would be swept into the sea. As a result Reuters emerged as the only international agency based in Tel Aviv and the hero of the Israelis. It was duly handed over, free of charge, to a consortium of local papers that had agreed to take it on and who gave it the new name of Itim.[2] In return, Reuters received a contract to supply foreign news against a regular payment in sterling, plus access to the domestic news reports from Itim. The office, equipment and staff were all transferred, working as before, to the new owner.

When Chancellor decided to sell the one-third stake in the German commercial news agency, Vereinigte Wirtschaftdienst (VWD), the retreat appeared wholesale. But he was thwarted by a mistake, made by a young accountant, Nigel Judah, who went on to become the current Finance Director of Reuters, and by Alfred Geiringer, then in charge of the commercial services. Judah added a nought to the price in German marks to be presented to VWD as the price for the shares. No one spotted the change among the welter of foreign currencies processed each month but Geiringer knew that the German partners would not accept the price and so the VWD stake was saved.

The policy of moving out of long-term commitments also meant a reduction of assets held by the company. Julius Reuter had laid his own telegraph cables to provide the communications essential for his business. Reuters now rented telegraphic circuits or radio transmitters from the appropriate government agency. Offices were rented, including the headquarters building in Fleet Street which belonged to the Press Association. The only equipment needed to keep a news agency going was a standard typewriter that could stand up to continuous battering.

Chancellor's austerity campaign to reduce the agency's commitments worked, but at a price. By allowing national news agencies to filter the Reuter news, the 'Reuter' credit at the end of each news item gradually disappeared in a growing number of newspapers around the world, to be replaced by the name of the local agency. Nevertheless, new subscribers were added and Reuters even broke into the American market to provide a minor and additional source of information. By the end of World War Two, over forty newspapers and radio stations in the US were taking the Reuters service.

On July 11, 1951, a thousand guests celebrated Reuters' centenary in a banquet at London's Grosvenor House Hotel. The Prime Minister and the Archbishop of Canterbury were among them. The guest of honour was Kent Cooper, executive head of the Associated Press, now Reuters' 'greatest ally'. Also present was William Haley, who had gone to the United States to pave the way for Chancellor's contractual talks with the Associated Press and to retrieve the situation following Cooper's row with Jones over AP's invasion of Japan eighteen years before. Haley had volunteered to smooth down Cooper. He had hung about for a whole month while Cooper refused to see him. When the two finally met, Cooper poured out his venom and rage for two hours. But Haley's cool reaction had a positive effect; the atmosphere eventually changed and the two ended up close friends.

The euphoria of the celebrations was complemented by the gradual withdrawal of wartime restrictions in the United Kingdom. Guests to the centenary visited the Festival of Britain and would soon report Churchill's return as Prime Minister. But beyond the pomp there lay the stark circumstances of the agency's balance sheet. In 1950, Reuters had managed a profit of £274 on a turnover of £1.2 million. The £25,000 budget for the centenary was overspent by just nine pounds ten shillings; but still the agency slipped £8,124 into the red that year.

Under Chancellor, the company see-sawed in and out of profit. No dividends were declared or expected; profit was not seen as a good thing in itself. Since the signing of the 1941 Trust it was accepted that Reuters was a 'non-profit-making organisation', a phrase repeated in Government memos and official company declarations. There was plenty of doublethink in the Trust and in the aspirations of the management after the war. With a securely based ownership, Reuters' aim was no longer to fly the British flag abroad, as under Jones: it was to embody the American philosophy of 'truth in news' and provide the best news service in the world. But this could only be sustained by making a profit and the strictures of the Trust appeared a formidable constraint. Over the years, this contradiction was to become more glaring and was only partially resolved when the company moved into substantial profit through the rapid expansion of its computerised commercial services.

Reuters had the advantage that Britain was still central to many of the main news stories of the day. In the late 1940s and 1950s the withdrawal from former colonial possessions and a spate of military obligations kept Britain on the front page of newspapers across the globe. National Service meant thousands of British youngsters were deployed in the Malayan emergency, the Korean War, the Singapore race riots, the Mau-Mau uprising in Kenya, the Suez débâcle or policing in Cyprus. Advertising revenue for British newspapers was good and not affected by competition from television and radio. The press had the cash to keep their subscriptions rising to pay for more and better coverage of world affairs and for the home-town, human interest stories which sold newspapers. The French, too, were fighting their colonial wars and De Gaulle stood large on the European scene. And though the Cold War was setting in, Reuters slipped the first western correspondent into Peking.

For the foreign correspondent these were the golden years. Without television to bring blood into the sitting-room, the public depended for their hot news on written descriptions published under the byline of their famous reporters. But to have a man on the spot was one thing, to get his report back to London and in the newspaper's hands in time for publication was a different matter. All too often, the newspaper's star correspondent arrived too late. He was in the wrong place or his despatches arrived mangled by long-distance communications, were delayed and subsequently missed edition time.

In such cases, the newspaper all too often had to turn to the material appearing on the Reuters teleprinters, stitched together with any material from a newspaper's own sources and published under the byline of the newspaper's own correspondent. There was logic in this: the British newspapers owned Reuters, so the agency man was, in effect, their own.

If this was the general practice, accepted by all sides, the knock-on effect was that the Reuter credit at the foot of any story began to disappear in the British press at the same time that it was dropped from overseas papers. The British public, as newspaper readers, might have been forgiven for questioning Reuters' connection with foreign reporting when it appeared that most of the stories from abroad came from the newspapers' own sources. Only a careful examination of each paper would reveal that most of the story was, word for word, exactly the same in each paper. The unsung agency man, was, after all, supplying the guts of the story.

While the end product of a Reuters news story might be served up very differently by each newspaper according to its political or philosophical bent, the function of the news agency itself was clear. Directives were sent out from time to time which outlined what sort of news was important to subscribers. Essentially, news despatches had to be on subjects that the papers wanted to print, or process and print. The news agency was like a public utility delivering to consumers the purest possible water. Leaving aside the question of the different taste of water in different localities, the job of the agency was to guard against outside contamination. What the consumers, or the newspapers did with the product was up to them and outside the control of the news agency. All the legal agreements conceivable could not prevent newspapers selecting the part of a story that agreed with their particular taste and making that the highlight of their presentation, even if the end result was that the reader was led to infer something that was very different from the truth.

There was a side effect to this because other journalists in Fleet Street tended to look on Reuters' strictly factual but bland coverage of world affairs as lacking the spice and flavour of their own journals. Reuters correspondents, on the other hand, often felt frustrated that they could not put more colour, and perhaps their own informed opinions, into the stories they wrote. Sandy Gall in his autobiography[3] describes it as 'an extraordinary anonymous occupation'. Edward Behr, who also started his journalistic career in the immediate post-war period, pins it down more precisely. His first written offering was rejected with the comment: 'We're not the London *Times*, remember', while his second effort brought a rebuke from the editor in charge who said: 'I don't know where you're from but you must remember we're not the *News of the World*'.[4]

The slashing of any financial commitments also affected the number of foreign correspondents employed by Reuters. By the early 'fifties Reuters had no home-based staff correspondents in the entire southern hemisphere. There were no Reuters staffers permanently based in all Latin America. There were no Reuters staffers in the entire African continent.

On the surface this policy was viable for two reasons. In the first place, world news was still dominated by news of the Great Powers and by colonial wars. What happened in the United States and in Europe was what was most important to the subscribers paying for

Reuters' service. Colonial wars would be staffed for as long as they lasted. And, secondly, news from other centres such as Israel or India was written or checked by individuals who had worked for the agency when it was owned or controlled by Reuters. They knew the standards and the style required, and more often than not they knew the editor who handled their area in London.

For the new generation of Reuters correspondents such as Edward Behr it seemed that no news was original Reuter material. Every news item was a rewrite of something written by someone else. Sent to work in Paris, Behr noted that 'In London, Agence France Presse (AFP) correspondents rewrote Reuters' copy, as fast as they could, and the finished product ended up as part of the AFP news service. In Paris we shamelessly rewrote Agence France Press copy serving it up as Reuters' fare. All over the world lesser news agencies were writing up their versions of Reuters stories and serving them as authentic Indian, Spanish or Brazilian news agency stories.'[5]

There was another reason why the system of depending on raw material from other agencies worked. The basic concept of any Reuters news story was that it had to be factually correct. The emphasis was on facts. Embellishment of any kind, whether it was humour, opinion or even interpretation, was not well considered. This had its roots in the days when it cost £20 to send ten words across the Atlantic by cable and it was enough to know which side had won the battle. With these sorts of costs it was not considered necessary or commercial to find out whether Wellington was the better general or whether Napoleon could not concentrate because of his piles.

The dependence on copy from other news agencies also had a firm contractual basis. Since the publication of the Reuters Trust agreement the agency was anxious to advertise its independence and also to ensure that other agencies were similarly bound. Reuters was now flourishing in all its contracts a new preamble of independence which usually went along the following lines: 'Both parties to this present agreement declare that they are news agencies serving no other purpose than the dissemination of truthful unbiased news, that they are free from any government or tendentious control and that the news which they supply to each other shall be compiled and selected purely on its merits as news and that editorial discretion on each side is free from outside dictation or pressure.'[6]

While such a commitment was perfectly acceptable for many of the news agencies with which Reuters had contracts it was clearly nonsense to expect that it had any relevance for the growing number that were controlled in one way or another by a particular government, party or individual.

As the 'fifties drew to a close Chancellor decided to leave Reuters and accept a new challenge in Fleet Street, as chairman of Odhams Press which published the loss-making *Daily Herald* and the profitable *Sunday People*. Despite his knighthood and international success, he was comparatively unknown at home. And, after eighteen years in the top job, he was getting bored. His deputy, Tony Cole, lured from the Press Association by William Haley during the war, was ambitious to take over. Cole had made his name as night editor at the PA working sixteen hours a day, often single-handed, to produce the news service for British papers. He was also the first chief executive trained outside Reuters as a journalist. An eighteen-stone Scotsman with enormous energy, he travelled the world with Chancellor, selling the Reuters service, and kept going by copious quantities of soda water on the way. The two first met by chance one night in 1941 when Cole stopped outside the entrance to Reuters' headquarters and picked up a rifle that Private Chancellor had dropped while lacing up the oversize boots he wore as a Home Guard sentry.

On July 1, 1959, Cole inherited an organisation which gave him the same sort of powers that Jones had used. The board members had rotated with the years and deferred to Chancellor as the individual who knew more than they and had kept the company on an even financial keel. There was no permanent chairman of the board, and even the title of chairman of the Reuters Trust had been dropped in 1953 when the original trust articles had been supplemented. The organisation was marked by very tight central control and every decision concerning costs was referred to the chief executive. Decisions on all fifty-three trading centres had to be approved by him. Cole took over a news agency still with a worldwide reputation, no financial fat, but increasingly vulnerable to the superior resources of both the American and the French agencies. In the end it killed him.

9

BOOTSTRAPS

'The most important thing is survival.'

—Gerald Long

When Tony Cole took over as general manager, he took the unusual step of combining the post with editor. In the past, the two jobs had ben kept separate; but Cole was a journalist to his fingertips and he would tell senior staff who aspired to his chair: 'You'll never be editor while I am alive.'

Cole made sure he was number one reporter in the agency: not for him the social whirl of the Jones era. Within a year of becoming general manager, he became the first news agency head to visit post-war China. After interviewing Mao Tse Tung, he sped back across the border to Hong Kong, disposed of two half-pound bars of chocolate and then dictated a 3,000-word exclusive story which was printed by every subscriber around the world.

Such scoops, though brilliant examples of adventurous, individual journalism, merely exposed the flaws elsewhere in Reuters' reporting network. In South Africa, for example, the delicate local operation had run into difficulties, pressurised by the Nationalist government and caught in the crossfire between the liberally inclined, British-controlled English-language press and the state monopoly South African Broadcasting Corporation (SABC). When police killed and wounded more than 250 Africans at the mining township of Sharpeville, the reports sent to London by the South African Press Association (SAPA) were incompetent and one-sided. And yet Reuters had to rely on SAPA, and its name and reputation were synonymous with the organisation. When subscribers' complaints began to mount, Reuters had to rush its own man out to Johannesburg to set up base for reporting southern Africa. Meanwhile, the local South African manager of Reuters commercial services was brought back to London to be 're-educated'.

Reuters' efforts to handle the complicated political situation in South Africa had already blown up once in its face, despite Chancellor's efforts to ensure the delicate local operation did not run into difficulty. His own family contacts meant he had plenty of friends there – his father had been the first Governor of Southern Rhodesia, and before that Governor of Mauritius, now an offshore holiday island for South Africans. On Chancellor's last goodwill visit, he was dined by the Prime Minister in Cape Town and treated as a special guest by the Government. On his way back to England up the east coast, his boat stopped at Port Elizabeth and he chatted at the rail with an old friend, the editor of the local paper. Unfortunately, some stinging comments about the Government's attitude to blacks were overheard by a hovering reporter who promptly relayed them to the SABC. The state radio broadcast them around the country and back to London, creating a diplomatic incident. Reuters embarrassed the Government even further when the Prime Minister lunched at their offices in Fleet Street. On that occasion the waiter asked Dr Malan how he would like his coffee. 'Hot and sweet, just like our women,' replied the Prime Minister. 'Yes sir,' said the waiter deadpan, 'black or white?'[1]

The public row with South Africa was no bad thing for Reuters' development in the rest of Africa. As the independence movements gathered strength, it was clear that they would demand more control of their information sources and outlets. The new leaders wanted the status symbols of independence: an airline, a steel mill, perhaps a new capital or port, but above all a government radio station and a news agency. These were the symbols of progress, but also real instruments of power because they gave the new leaders the ability to control the news and propaganda flow within their own countries.

Cole commissioned Patrick Crosse, one of the most senior Reuters staffers and then in charge of Italy and the Vatican reporting, to look at how Reuters should tackle the independence movement in Africa. There was no question of the new indigenous African news agencies being co-operatives owned by the local press – the Reuters model – because in many cases no substantial local press existed. Crosse hit on the idea of a national news agency for each newly independent country with back-up training supplied by Reuters. It was no easy task, for few if any of the former European colonies in Africa had any concept of the principles of independent reporting as drawn up in the Reuters Trust. But it offered at least the opportunity for Reuters to keep a toehold in these nascent states at a time of upheaval.

Similar wholesale arrangements were made with the communist countries which would not permit direct distribution of news by western agencies to their own press and radio. They often refused to pay for the service at all. China denied even receiving it, although it was obvious Peking picked up the radio signals transmitted from London. The Soviet Union insisted on the principle of 'reciprocity', which meant that the agencies swapped their news services without payment on either side. Reuters argued that its own news service was worth more and that a differential payment should reflect this. However, for the commercial services Reuters signed contracts with the Russians and the Chinese – and got paid in sterling. Competition from the French and the American agencies meant that wholesale buyers like the Japanese or the Indians were able to squeeze subscriptions to levels which bore no relation to the going rate in the private sector. In many counties where Reuters was allowed to distribute news locally, the costs of working in another language nevertheless made it commercially impossible. Across the breadth of Europe, with the exception of France, throughout the Middle East and Africa, across most of Asia, including Japan and even down to Australasia, Reuters was now dealing with the local press at one remove.

For the present, Reuters had to finance any development by hauling itself up by its own bootstraps. The tireless sales trips of Tony Cole and his tight-fisted control of costs forced the profit figures to creep up. In 1961 profits nearly touched £40,000 on sales of £2.7 million. It was becoming evident that what Reuters did best was what Reuters did itself. In South-East Asia, a tough Australian called Graham Jenkins, with none of the hang-ups of the British in a colonial climate, was changing radically the way in which the British news agency operated and the good news was reflected in the profits.

Viewed against its high reputation and how it was later to expand, the scale of operations in South-East Asia was tiny. After World War Two, the headquarters had moved to Hong Kong but then shifted down to Singapore. These two colonies, with their strong English-language newspapers and their large commercial communities, were the mainstay of revenue in the area.

In Singapore, the balance of power, both political and commercial, was fast swinging away from the colonial civil servants and the great British trading houses that had dominated the colony since the days of Sir Stamford Raffles. The new Reuters manager, Jenkins, opted out of the 'whites only' Tanglin club set and concentrated on rebuilding the shabby Reuters offices, installing unheard of luxuries like air-conditioning. His efforts to reform the work routines took longer and provoked a hostile response from the Chinese staff who ran the day-to-day administration.

Since the Europeans had begun trading in the Far East it had been the custom to employ a local Chinese to run the office. He in turn took on the necessary staff. The advantage was that the Europeans did not have to bother about routine administration, nor master the language. Wage negotiations were simple. It was only necessary to deal with one individual; the rest were his relations and they paid him a percentage of their wages for their jobs.

The system irritated Jenkins who wanted control over the accounting system; he wanted to know how much he was paying for each item and he needed to be sure that the commercial news reports produced by the Chinese reporters were accurate. While Jenkins could be as smooth as any Australian diplomat when he wanted to be, and was often mistaken for the film star William Holden, he was about as gentle as a rattlesnake. His verbal assaults were terrifying. Foam flew from his mouth as he stormed at some miscreant who finally fled, relieved that he had not been strangled. Jenkins would then turn round to anyone present and say with a big grin, completely calm, 'That should fix him for a week or two'.

The main target for his rage was the Chinese manager, See Gim Hock, who resisted all the more strongly because he had all his Chinese relations solidly behind him. Cole, still deputy to Chancellor at the time, became drawn into the fight and was finally persuaded to referee the showdown. When he visited Singapore in 1955, he stayed at the Cathay Hotel where a suite had been booked. Jenkins invited See to the hotel and confronted him with an ultimatum on how the office was to be organised in future. In the next room, Cole knelt at a crack in the door to make sure there were no misunderstandings.[2]

With See Gim Hock's power broken, Jenkins was able to modernise in earnest. New machinery was bought, revolutionary offset litho printing presses installed, and uniforms designed for the messengers in the colours favoured by the first Baron Reuter – confederate grey and royal blue.

From his revamped headquarters Jenkins produced a new regional service targeted at the surrounding countries. Singapore also acted as the funnel through which news from the area was relayed to London, although many of the stories filed by local correspondents were purely for regional distribution and not intended to be part of the world news file. The reason for the regional file was economic. Jenkins anticipated the pressure from Third World countries for news devoted to their own activities, and he felt that a high local content would make for a far more acceptable and saleable service for newspaper and radio stations in South-East Asia.

It was Jenkins, too, who forced the pace over the indigenisation of key posts. Across the causeway in Malaya, the *merdeka* or independence celebrations preceded those in Singapore and Jenkins risked promoting a Malay teleprinter operator from Singapore to be the first Asian manager in the newly independent state. Jenkins also removed a young Korean, Jimmy Hahn, from his previous post in Hong Kong and made him local staff correspondent. Hahn had escaped from communist Shanghai, where his father had been a textile millionaire, and he had bribed his way into Hong Kong. Without a penny, he lived on a rented shelf in the ghettoes of the colony before talking himself into a job as a Reuters messenger. He quickly climbed the promotion ladder, moved to Singapore, and by 1964 took over as the first Asian manager for South-East Asia and the first non-European to hold a senior executive position in the news agency.[3]

The efforts of Jenkins in Singapore showed how resourceful and adaptable the agency had become, suffering none of the listlessness and complacency which affected many other British companies abroad. It was this same enormous strength and vitality within the agency which was to enable it to transform its fortunes ten years later.

South-East Asia was a model for the way Reuters was changing slowly into a commercial force to be reckoned with. Of course, progress was often slow. When the French colonial administration left South Vietnam in the wake of the defeat at Dienbienphu, Reuters moved in. The South controlled what had once been the rice bowl of Asia and one of the main goals of the government was to revitalise the paddy fields and the rubber plantations to feed the country and to pay for imports. Here was a chance to sell key price information to the Ministry of Commerce and in due course a trial service started.

It was housed in a government building, above the room where the national orchestra practised playing western national anthems on their traditional instruments. Clerks were trained to decode the messages, translators briefed to produce the service in French, and a motorised trishaw was arranged each night to visit the government reception station with a small gift of cigarettes to ensure the operator woke up and tuned into the right radio signals. But the trial service flopped, a result not of the quality but divisions within the British news agency.

The correspondent in Saigon, Jacques Mootoosamy, was a former sergeant in French Intelligence from the island of Reunion in the Indian Ocean. Mootoosamy was not the sort of man to inspire confidence in a country that had just got rid of the French military and he was not Reuters' first choice. Hired originally as number two and local 'fixer', he had taken over when the end of the war meant the story did not merit the costs of a London-based staff correspondent. When the time came for a decision on the commercial contract, the Minister concerned sent for the correspondent and the individual appointed to run the trial service. He said he could not understand why both men's assessment of the contract was so different. The Minister produced a sheaf of cables from his drawer: 'We make seven copies of all cables sent by journalists,' he said. 'In my position in the Cabinet I get the second copy.'[4]

If Vietnam was a failure, there were successes elsewhere. Reuters had operated a tiny but profitable office in Thailand for many years, but in neighbouring Burma it had been impossible to make any progress in a country that had nationalised most forms of business activity. Jenkins took an office just 103 steps of tropical heat up one of the old and virtually empty colonial trading houses. The flat roof was suitable for the antennae needed to receive the signals from Singapore and soon a small service started by hand delivery to the local newspapers and state trading firms. Typical was the response of the chairman of the nationalised concern that handled the country's rice production. 'We are doing very well this year,' he told the Reuters manager. 'We should have a good surplus for the first time in several years. Now, can you tell me how to go about selling it abroad?'[5]

Most of Jenkins' Asian recruits were the usual unflappable and unemotional type – but not all. When the Reuters manager in Rangoon visited the number two at the Ministry of Information, U Thaung Myine, to offer the Burmese a job, he found him holding half a telephone in his hand. 'You know,' said the Burmese very quietly, pointing to the shattered pieces on the floor, 'some people can make me very irritated.'

At the other end of South-East Asia, in the Philippines, the market economy boomed. There were no shortages that money could not fix. There were not just nightclubs, but 'day and night clubs' that never closed. Manila had the largest ballroom in Asia which fielded a thousand dancers; and it had the largest bar, a hundred feet of solid hardwood. Signs in offices and restaurants proclaimed 'leave your firearms with the cashier', but few did.

During the war, the Reuters manager, Alan Hammond, and other foreign correspondents were interned in a Japanese concentration camp. The man from the Associated Press had toiled loyally as the invading armies marched into Manila. Minutes before he was captured, the last cable arrived from head office in New York. No sympathy or congratulations. It simply read: 'ex-accounts. need urgentest details personal tax return'.[7]

When the war ended, Hammond went back to England and the

news service was restarted by an English businessman, Peter Richards, who ran it as a franchise. He was a great socialiser and contacts man, spending every evening at one party or another. He used to claim that his Spanish wife, Dolly, had not had to make dinner for four years.

Richards built up a small and loyal team which he handed over to Reuters in 1958 so that he could move to Spain. The business continued under the Reuters name and produced both bulletins for commercial clients and a service for the local newspapers that published in English, Spanish and Chinese. One of the staffers, Leo Gonzaga, coached his local basketball team in the suburbs and travelled in every night to the office by bus. At about three o'clock one morning, the Reuters correspondent got a call from Gonzaga to ask if he could come to the office urgently. He found the Filipino doubled up with pain, an arm in a sling, trying to type with one hand. Gonzaga had gone to sleep on the bus with his arm out of the window, when the bus had side-swiped a tree. 'I can manage to get the summaries done,' he said, nursing a broken arm, 'it's just that I can't type them quickly enough. Can you help?'[8]

Each of the regional offices, with the exception of Burma which could not get the required government permission, transmitted a daily news service to Singapore. From there it was tacked on to the world news from London and retransmitted as the regional news service. Apart from Singapore, the most sophisticated office was in Hong Kong. Here Reuters catered for the multilingual newspaper community and even produced a small news service in Chinese. Wall Street was beginning its first post-war boom and the local brokers wanted American stock exchange prices delivered each morning. As the New York prices arrived during the night they were quickly decoded and ferried to the printshop of an elderly Indian who set them by hand in lead for printing on an ancient flatbed press.

As Jenkins and Reuters' New Zealand manager in Hong Kong, Ian McCrone, found out, it was vital to sort out conditions on the ground if the news agency was to function properly. It was a painstaking process, as difficult as the business of controlling and adapting to Reuters' core cost and technical problem: communications.

As the 'fifties drew to a close a new generation of international cables were laid which offered a drastic improvement over radio. The earlier advantage of radio transmission was that one transmitter could serve any number of receivers within the range of its signals. The more receivers tuned in, the more cost-effective the signal. But on certain routes, such as London-New York, it was more important to shift vast numbers of words and numbers quickly, rather than serve additional points.

The new cables offered a higher degree of reliability than shortwave transmissions, bedevilled by interruptions and breaks which always seemed to occur at critical times. In 1960, Reuters leased its first transatlantic cable circuit, the forerunner of many such continental links. The agency had already taken a direct line to Paris in 1945, and, gradually, landlines spanned out within each country where Reuters operated. By 1950, a teleprinter network linked the main European news centres.

The first real breakthrough in making more efficient use of cables came three years after tentatively leasing the first transatlantic circuit. The invention of transistors, with their miniature size, had transformed the world of communications. In 1963, Reuters upgraded the quality of its transatlantic circuit from one sufficient to carry teleprinter signals to one able to carry voice, or telephone traffic. Equipment was put into this line which enabled the circuit to be split into twenty-two teleprinter channels in each direction, forty-four circuits in all. By the following year, even that was out of date and a new system was introduced which doubled the capacity to forty-four duplex channels.

Packing more information into a given circuit was no longer a question of the company secretary working out complicated codes in his study at home. Bright young engineers were now devoting months to design equipment that was out of date even before it was installed. By the end of the decade, Reuters was leasing the equivalent of nearly two million miles of teleprinter line. Ten years later, even that figure was insignificant.

The increase in communications capacity across the Atlantic enabled Reuters to have another shot at the toughest market of all: Latin America, for long the scene of successive defeats and withdrawals for the agency. Even with Government money, Jones had failed, and Chancellor had made another effort when he took over the French agency offices during World War Two. The problems were twofold. In the first place, Latin American newspapers, with a few key exceptions, did not value foreign news sufficiently highly to pay much in subscriptions. Besides, they could choose from a number of agencies that offered cut-rate services. Furthermore, because of South America's geographical position, it was much cheaper and more effective to beam a radio signal from North America or Canada rather than from a point in the United Kingdom.

Reuters had kept a toehold in Argentina, Brazil and Chile; it had even employed a retired British consul from Mendoza, in

Argentina, to lay telephone lines across the roofs of Buenos Aires for connection to commercial subscribers. This was illegal but normal practice in the absence of official lines and several enterprising people helped companies on a full-time basis laying lines which government inspectors from time to time intercepted and cut. One day, while reeling out a line above the business district in the fashionable Florida Street, the Reuters linesman took a step backwards and fell four storeys to his death.

Poor communications may have been one reason for the near bankruptcy of Reuters' reputation in Latin America by the early 'sixties. In Mexico City, the foreign editor of *The Excelsior* newspaper was asked to subscribe to a new service: 'I remember Reuters. We took your service during the war. You had a story one day saying that Hess (Hitler's deputy) had been discovered in Ploughman, England,' he said, referring to the wayward report. 'Your American friends gave us 350 words on how Hess was found by a ploughman after he had parachuted into Scotland. We don't trust your news.'[9]

In Chile, Agustin Edwards, the owner of the leading newspaper of the country, *El Mercurio*, whose family had brought cricket to Chile and who sent his children to school in England, was equally blunt. 'I am not going to give Reuters a contract. We shall take your service but you will only have my word for it. I keep my word. And that is worth more than a Reuters contract.'[10]

The foreign editor and member of the owning family of Brazil's largest newspaper, *O Estado de Sao Paulo*, was even more bitter. 'The last news item we published about Reuters was a little box on the front page with the heading "The Shame of Reuters",' said Ruy Mesquita. 'Your manager came down from New York, telephoned us to say that the contract for the news service was cancelled, put the key to the office in his pocket and took the next plane back to New York.'[11]

Technology, in the form of cheaper and faster transatlantic teleprinter circuits, would bring Reuters a lot closer to Latin America. It was a market the agency could not afford to ignore, but as Tony Cole fought for the company's survival, the example of Reuters' own operation in South-East Asia was more valuable. He looked at the relative richness of continental Europe and its contributions to the Reuters balance sheet. In the autumn of 1962, he decided on a bold gamble. Apart from France where Reuters had always had its own office, the rest of Europe was farmed out to national or private news agencies which distributed the Reuters news and commercial services. The agencies were more or less well situated according to how the press of each country treated them.

Some were very badly placed and kept very short of money. Reuters needed revenue urgently and could not afford the big-hearted generosity of supporting a whole family of little 'Reuters' in Europe. There seemed to be no possibility that Reuters would get substantially large amounts of cash through these agencies and, even if the agencies themselves raised more revenue, it was highly unlikely they were going to hand it over. It was, in effect, a guarantee of slow strangulation.

Cole chose what appeared to be the weakest link and, for Reuters, the most advantageous point: Belgium. The choice was a warning shot to all the European agencies, for the Belga agency was a founder member of what was known as the '39 Group, the collective name for the European agencies that had banded together that year to ensure the continuation of free exchange and non-competition between friendly agencies. The war wrecked the international cartel, but the '39 Group expanded afterwards to include the agencies of nine other European agencies including Britain's Press Association. The main activity of the '39 Group now consisted of club meetings which exchanged information on developments in communications.

Cole told Belga that Reuters had decided to distribute its own commercial services. But he was cautious. Despite his outgoing personality and his image as a salesman of genius, he realised his knowledge of the commercial services was minimal. To spearhead the operation he chose a young Australian, Glen Renfrew, who had joined the agency in 1952. Cole was so unsure of himself that, even as Renfrew started up the new operation in the Rue Royale in Brussels, he offered the job to two other people.

Cole sent as his personal emissary Gerald Long, one of his assistant general managers, with a brief to check on everything that Renfrew did and to make sure that the European news agency boat was not rocked. Long's grasp of the commercial services was as weak as Cole's. Renfrew spotted this quickly and banished him, in Australian language, to the house he had rented in what he fondly called the 'Avenue des Vagabondes'.[12]

The head of the Belgian agency, Daniel Ryelandt, was in a cleft stick. He was faced with a demand for increased fees for the Reuters general news service at the same time as his capacity to pay was diminished by his loss of commercial service revenue. In desperation he decided on a personal appeal to Cole. When he arrived in Fleet Street he was met by Cole's personal assistant, Robert Elphick. Cole was stricken with flu, but that day had made a special effort to come to the office. When Elphick went in to alert his boss, he found him dead on the sofa.[13]

10

INSTANT MONEY

'We created a market for foreign exchange where none existed
before.'   —Official Reuters publicity material.

Twenty-one steps and a generation of technology separate Reuters
from its former owners, the Press Association. Scattered around Fleet
Street and the surrounding area, the London newspapers who came to
partner the PA in 1941 fight their personal and public feuds with
machinery largely of another age. Not so far away in Gray's Inn Road,
journalists at *The Sunday Times* chain their manual typewriters to
their desks lest these valuable tools of the trade are pinched.

On the fourth floor at Reuters, the editor in charge checks his
personal screen for movements of correspondents around the
world, notes internal announcements area by area, scans regional
news files and worries that the translation of a key story distributed
in German from Bonn is faster than the same version issued in
English from London. As the day ends in Fleet Street and the
morning papers are put to bed, the duty editor at Reuters hands
over control of the world news file to his colleague in Hong Kong
who edits the 'night world' on the other side of the globe. The news
flow remains the same. Distance is no object, only the cost of
making sure communications are that much sharper than competitors. From a worn-out news agency with no future, Reuters has
pulled itself up so far over thirty years that the reality matches the
reputation. How did this transformation come about when the
owners begrudged every penny of their subscription fees and the
agency watched its home base in London lose out to the United
States as the centre of communications and finance?

It was perhaps fitting that the seeds of Reuters' future prosperity
should be sown in Germany just a year after the company concluded
its expensive centenary celebrations. It was from Germany that the
young Julius Reuter fled in 1848 and it was here that he returned to
start his first short but successful pigeon news service. In 1952,
Christopher Chancellor called a meeting with his deputy, Tony
Cole, and an enthusiastic Austrian, Alfred Geiringer, in the spa
town of Bad Godesberg, just outside Bonn.

Back in 1947, Geiringer had met a young British army officer stationed in Dusseldorf. He was struck by the officer's fluent German and by his enthusiasm for a local performance of a then comparatively unknown play, *Danton's Death* by Georg Büchner. The officer's name was Gerald Long. When he told Geiringer he was interested in journalism, Geiringer suggested they meet when Long was demobilised.[1] It was to prove an inspired catch.

In the immediate post-war reorganisation of Western Germany, Geiringer set up five main reporting offices for Reuters and started distributing a news service to local newspapers. As Reuters' finances suffered, Geiringer put together a new German news agency by combining the Deutsche Presse Dienst (DPD) which operated in the British zone and the DENA agency in the American zone into the new Deutsche Presse Agentur (DPA). The new agency took over the Reuter contracts, providing Reuters with a news report from Germany and a regular payment in sterling. Chancellor offered Geiringer a fresh challenge: take over and reorganise Reuters commercial services which were only just re-emerging as a potential source of significant revenue.

Geiringer suggested to Chancellor that they resurrect the name of a dormant British company owned by Reuters and which no longer traded in Britain. This was a small private company based in Liverpool called the Commercial Telegram Bureau, trading under the name of Comtelburo, which Chancellor bought in 1943 for £30,000. It used to enjoy a virtual monopoly of reporting commercial prices between Britain and South America and it also had an office in North America in downtown New York. Wartime, the lack of communications and the stagnation of world markets, had all but finished the company. The last family owner shot himself in a Sao Paulo hotel.[2]

Geiringer suggested revitalising the commercial service by operating it independently under the Comtelburo name. The company would have its own board of directors headed by Chancellor and Cole; it would also provide a new focus for the energy, loyalty and, hopefully, profits that the service would generate. Cole was lukewarm. He distrusted Geiringer's ambitions and suspected that the real reason for Geiringer's proposal was that the Austrian wanted to work independently and report directly to Chancellor, bypassing him as the effective chief of operations.

Chancellor, however, went along with Geiringer's proposals and also with another of his suggestions. The early post-war years showed Chancellor the weakness among the old guard of foreign correspondents he had inherited from Jones. Many were more suited to the cocktail circuit than to the hard grind of chasing and writing news stories. By the early 1950s he enlisted the help of the Appointments Board at his old university, Cambridge, and recruited bright young graduates who were willing to work for the sort of pittance that Reuters paid. Geiringer asked Chancellor if he could do the same thing and secured a reluctant agreement. Asked by Chancellor how many people he wanted to hire, Geiringer replied, 'About a dozen to start with', and promptly trailed off to the Appointments Board.

Among the early recruits for the revamped Comtelburo Ltd. were an Oxford graduate, Michael Nelson, and a young accountant, Nigel Judah, loaned for a few months to Geiringer by Cole. Both were to play vital roles in the agency's development. At the same time, an Australian, fresh off the boat from Sydney University, had the temerity to knock on Reuters' door and ask for a job. Taken on by Geiringer to work on trial for half the normal rate, Glen Renfrew eventually asked to see his boss and explained that he could not live on his pay. 'Alright,' said Geiringer in his guttural English, 'I can give you a few more pounds – a year.' The increase, when it came, turned out to be 11/6d (equivalent to some 57 pence) a week.[3]

The new recruits soon learned that an absence of funds was no excuse for slow or incomplete reporting. There was a standard joke outside London about press conferences abroad: the man from the Associated Press would arrive in his chauffeur-driven car; the correspondent from United Press would come in his own car; the representative from Agence France Presse would hurtle in by taxi; and the chap from Reuters would arrive breathless, by bicycle, first. Cars were an almost impossible luxury for any correspondent. Only the manager for South-East Asia employed a driver, and that was because of the tropical heat. The chief representative in France could not drive. Accounts differ as to whether his driver worked part-time as a cabbie or whether it was a full-time cabbie who doubled up as a chauffeur. Either way, Reuters kept costs to a minimum.

By the time Gerald Long settled into his new job as general manager, the recruits taken on by Chancellor and Geiringer were coming on-stream. Geiringer himself left in 1958, unable to come to a working arrangement with Cole, largely because of Cole's suspicious nature and his desire to keep every activity under his own control.

One of Long's first acts was to make Nelson, recently appointed sole manager of the commercial services, report to him direct. Long realised that the only way for the agency to improve and expand the quality of the general reporting for the media was to expand the profits of the commercial services. He allowed Nelson to plough back a small percentage of the profits into expansion instead of using the commercial services as a milch cow for the media services. Obvious though this seemed in retrospect, the decision to allow the commercial services to reinvest some £27,000 of its own money was not considered the done thing by many members of Reuters' establishment. The division between the news service bridge and the commercial service engine room had grown wider since the days of Jones and Chancellor, and it was not diminished by the new generation of graduates; far from it, they were now the ones most likely to be at loggerheads. Long himself noted that if some Reuters correspondents were asked to do a report for the commercial services, or Comtel for short, they simply refused.[4]

What Long was later to call this 'loony' attitude was central to the whole problem faced by Reuters: money. The Reuters Trust had shouted to the world that the news agency was a non-profit-making organisation. Business was about making profits and, *ergo*, Reuters was not a business. The money propping up Reuters came from the splendid intellectual pursuits of producing newspapers and any digression from that aim was out of the question. The blandishments of commerce, as well as those of government, were decried in equal measure. And so an unhealthy rivalry for funds grew up between the news and commercial arms of Reuters. It was to plague Long's tenure as chief executive.

When Long moved into his corner office on the seventh floor of the PA-Reuters building, he made appointments to see the press barons of Fleet Street, effectively his bosses. One of them was very open: 'Your costs are increasing and will increase enormously. The money you need to run a world news service you won't get from the owners – they won't pay. The only alternative is to take very large sums of money from the British Government.'[5] At that time inflation was relatively insignificant, and Long could see the logic in what he was told. But he felt it was repugnant: it meant returning to the schemes put up by Roderick Jones, something he had no intention of doing. The only way to survive was to become an out-and-out commercial operation.

When Long took over in 1963 the survival of Reuters was by no means certain. The great lesson the news agency learnt in South-East Asia and Belgium was that it could do far better on its own than working through others. Chancellor's investment in people was paying off and the practical developments in communications gave the spark to move ahead faster.

Long's determination to have his own way started in an un-dramatic fashion. He stopped referring to the board many of the minutiae the directors had come to expect but which he considered to be management's responsibility. The authority given to him by the board was nebulous, so Long decided himself how much he wanted to take. His appointment to the top job came as a surprise to him as much as it did to his competitors and the rest of the agency's employees. He gave no indication of future great ex-pectations when he took the night train from Brussels back to London on the evening of January 26, 1963, the day after Tony Cole had died, literally in office. The board interviewed all the likely candidates and only one person outside Reuters. Michael King, the son of the boss of Mirror Newspapers, Cecil King, had to be sneaked through the back door into the Savoy Hotel door for his private interview. When the board summoned Long and asked him if he wanted the job, he was speechless for a full minute, until prompted by the chairman, Sir John Burgess, who said: 'Come on, man, do you want it or not?'[6]

Outwardly an intellectual snob, Long applied all his consider-able intellectual power to any problem he faced, whether it was dominating the board, dealing with trade unions or discussing his consuming passion, food. He had an incisive mind. But when it came to dealing with people, he displayed strange prejudices. He took the credit for persuading the highly organised Reuters unions in London to follow each step of the computerisation programme, but in negotiations he displayed a truculent and impatient manner. He preferred to let others get on with the detail. When he left Reuters to take on the job of rebuilding Times Newspapers and came face to face with the stormtrooping élite of the Fleet Street unions, he had nothing to offer. The fact was that he had set up a malleable personnel machine at Reuters which did not move with him to Gray's Inn Road.

Every penny that Long diverted to strengthen the commercial services meant, or at least implied, a penny less for the budget for reporting general news. The shoe was now on the other foot and it was the so-called intelligentsia who cried poverty and demanded a larger cut from the profits that the commercial services were generating. The seeds of division had taken root in Roderick Jones' day and the two arms of Reuters were now divided by mistrust.

As the unusually cold winter of 1962/63 drew to an end, Michael Nelson could be found studying the results of a survey he had commissioned on the United States, where a brand new concept was challenging the established methods of commercial price reporting.

Though primitive by today's standards, the Stockmaster machine had three electronic eyes which flashed out price quotes on demand. Now a dealer in San Francisco could answer a client's question by punching out a series of coded buttons and know the price of Ford Motor Company in New York within an average of ten seconds.

It was clear that if Reuters was going to continue to offer the crucial time-edge to its subscribers then Reuters itself had to be first with the prices. Nelson's survey, produced by reputable experts and covering the whole of Europe, cost £3,000, an expensive investment at the time. It concluded that throughout the whole of continental Europe and the United Kingdom, Reuters might, eventually, be able to sell three or four of the new devices. That was the scope of the potential market. Nelson argued, successfully, that the survey's results vastly underestimated the market's potential and size. It could be said that this one commercial insight did more to influence the future of the agency than almost any other in the post-war period.

Until Stockmaster, most markets in the United States disseminated prices by what was generally called a ticker tape. In each stock or commodity exchange, operators would sit and type on to a machine, similar to a telex, the latest prices as they were marked on a chalk board above the trading floor. The ticker-tape signal was transmitted by telephone line to machines all over the country which printed out each price transaction as it was relayed. It was also projected on lights in brokers' dealing rooms where clients were invited to sit and watch the tape, and buy and sell stock and commodities.

Reuters also had similar tape machines in its offices in New York, Chicago and other key trading centres where clerks selected the prices needed for transmission to London where they were relayed to the rest of the world. The drawback of the ticker-tape system was that you had to sort through a bundle of paper and prices before you found the price you wanted. And the tape was often slow. When trading became hectic, the tape fell behind. Just when clients were clamouring to buy or sell, the dealers did not know the latest price to quote.

By early 1963, the American company which had developed Stockmaster, Ultronic Systems Corporation, moved its equipment into Europe to serve stockbrokers with whom it already had contracts in New York. Fortunately for Reuters the move failed. The reason was a combination of cost and speed. To provide prices to subscribers at an acceptable speed, the machine needed a wide bandwidth of communications down which to transmit the signals. The wider the bandwidth the more expensive the communications, and leasing transatlantic cable time was still astronomic in price.

It was at just this moment that Reuters was installing the first specialist equipment on its transatlantic cable circuit which allowed it to pack the equivalent of twenty-two teleprinter channels into one telephone channel. With the cost of its communications slashed and spare capacity now available, Reuters could install machines with acceptable speeds in Europe at prices the American stockbrokers could afford.

On July 1, 1964, Reuters introduced the new equipment into Europe, having signed up the rights to market Ultronic's price interrogation systems outside the United States. The individual selected by Reuters to take the news agency into the computer age was Glen Renfrew, the man who had kicked Long out of his Brussels office the year before. Renfrew's first task was to convince companies in Europe that it was worth paying for the new Stockmaster devices to be installed in their offices, even though they were more expensive than the comparable service in the United States. Renfrew had no one to help him: Reuters had at the time no salesmen. The burly Australian had to sell himself – literally – and, at the same time, grasp the complex technology underpinning the computer service.

The new quotation retrieval devices on the stockbroker's desk relied on a central computer which stored all the information received by various price tickers from distant markets. Stockmaster's attraction was this: it allowed a number of other machines at the end of a telephone line to interrogate it at the same time. Very soon it became obvious that, if a duplicate or 'slave' of the master computer in the United States were installed in London, subscribers would not have to wait for their questions and answers to be relayed across the Atlantic. Equally, with less traffic crossing the ocean, Reuters could cut capacity in the cable circuit. Since many firms were reluctant to pay $2,000 or more a month for equipment only useful for a few hours in the late afternoon when the North American markets were open, the commercial advantages of Reuters' new system were clear.

By 1967, Reuters' slave computer in London had become a 'master' in its own right. Prices from the various European stock and commodity exchanges were piped into it during the European working day, and London controlled in turn a succession of 'slaves' around Europe, each linked by cable and using the same technology that had been introduced across the Atlantic. As they proved their worth, more capacity was introduced on the Atlantic and a web of similar leased circuits started to snake out to Africa, the Far East and to Australia.

The disadvantage of the Stockmaster system and its early competitors in the price interrogation market was that it only covered prices and not news. The next generation of equipment, called Videomaster, corrected this by offering a whole selection of information presented on a television screen. It was now possible for a subscriber to alter the format of his own screen, within certain limits, to suit his personal requirements. But the system was still rigid and expensive to maintain.

In 1970, a small development team at Reuters came up with two ideas that were to change drastically the future profitability of the company. Peter Benjamin, head of Reuters' technical department, was the first to suggest abandoning the complicated 'hard-wire' system and move over to a software basis. This had two advantages: the same basic box and screen would be used, but by switching software and using plug-in boards at a subscriber's office, the selection and presentation of information shown on the screen could be changed. A quick visit by a technician would 'enable' or 'disable' a subscriber to retrieve specific information stored in the appropriate 'slave' computer to which he was connected. But above all, this ingenious solution allowed Reuters, for the first time, to develop its own equipment instead of buying from its American partner and paying a royalty on each piece of gear installed. It was, incidentally, the name of this partner, Ultronic Systems, which gave rise to press reports that Reuters was getting into the video games business. In fact, the American firm had nothing to do with Ultronic Ltd., a video games specialist located in London's Belgravia.

As Benjamin's ideas turned into reality, Nelson and Renfrew had a stroke of luck. A new commodity appeared on the scene. Unlike the conventional type of commodity which had become fashionable such as frozen orange juice, soya beans or propane, it was the very stuff that enabled commodities to be shifted around the world, to be bought and sold: money.

Reuters had been quoting exchange rates from the days of the first telegram service between London and Paris. But, since the end of World War Two, international exchange rates had been virtually frozen by the Bretton Woods Agreement. In December 1971, the arrangement finally collapsed, to be replaced by the Smithsonian Agreement which let the major world currencies find their own value against each other according to supply and demand in the world's market places.

Money was unique as a commodity in one very important respect. It was traditionally bought and sold by individuals over a telephone. There was no 'open cry' where dealers gathered together for fixed periods to shout themselves hoarse and establish prices that were subsequently recorded as official market prices. In other words, there was no physical market place for money.

Reuters had reported the movements of individual exchanges by telephoning key dealers and reporting what they considered to be an average of the opinions they contacted. As money rates started to move up and down in the same way as any other commodity, the volume of business started to grow. Commercial firms needed to protect overseas sales or imports against unfavourable movements of the currency. Speculators moved in, trying to out-guess everyone else and make a killing in the process, while the big pension funds saw the need to move into 'safe' currencies. In each case, their businesses depended on having fast, accurate and up-to-date information on the international money market.

It was only now that the flexibility of Benjamin's ideas really came into their own. In the absence of a market place where individuals could meet and fix prices, Reuters would 'invent' one. It would not be a building but a delicate composition of mircrochips and integrated circuits joined together by more than three million kilometres of leased communication circuits: the electronic market place.

The brains behind this new service was a former Reuters messenger, a cockney who had left school at fourteen and who would never have been considered suitable for employment by Reuters in the computer age. Fred Taylor had worked his way up to be a clerk on the lowly section that reported and coded London prices for transmission around the world and he had built up a range of contacts on the telephone. He had a good line in patter but, face to face, was curiously diffident and preferred to let others propose publicly the ideas that he had quietly gathered. He rarely met his powerful City of London contacts, turned down offers to spend weekends on exotic yachts and went back home to dig the small garden behind his council house in South London.

When the Bretton Woods Agreement began to crumble, Reuters turned to the banks in London and asked them about their needs for a future money service. The banks' answers proved that Fred Taylor's vision of an electronic market place was not as fanciful as it seemed. But not everyone agreed. One prominent executive at Barclay's Bank told Michael Nelson that the planned service would not last three months, though he agreed to subscribe. Another said it might eventually garner a maximum of 230 subscribers. It was engineered for a maximum of 250 and started on June 4, 1973, with a total of five.

The launch of the Reuters Monitor service involved more than a flood of lunches and fast recruitment of salesmen. Reuters needed to borrow money, more than it had ever borrowed before, to underwrite the costs of development and installation of the new equipment. Long put his job on the line for the loan from the banks of a million pounds, a huge sum for the company at the time. The board went along with Long, as it always did. But at times many of them, especially those from the provinces, became increasingly nervous at his forays in expensive gadgetry that seemed to have nothing to do with their own business of producing newspapers.

The Monitor service also had to overcome a formidable hurdle in the market. Essentially, it reversed the roles in price communication: instead of Reuters phoning a bank for a money rate, the bank itself inserted into the computer its own 'buy' and 'sell' prices for a range of given currencies. The drawback in this instant money game was that nobody was too keen on playing for real; it was like the 'dummy' in a game of bridge with all his cards exposed on screen and everyone else hiding behind their blank television monitors. Those who contributed data, the so-called 'market makers', would not pay to put their data into the system unless they felt there were sufficient people looking at the data who might come to them for business. Those who might want to buy or sell money would not pay to join unless enough 'market makers' showed their hands to provide a choice.

Despite these difficulties, the Money Monitor began to take off, boosted by the agency's biggest-ever publicity campaign and new salesmen recruited on what was for Reuters an unheard-of scale. By now the old telephone and telex market could not cope with the growth in money business, accelerated by inflation and the rising price of oil.

In Europe, Reuters kept the good news to itself. It had already proved in Belgium that it could operate the commercial service better independently rather than through the filter of local agencies. In 1967, another opportunity arose when the owner of the Swiss commercial agency which had distributed Reuters commercial services since 1945, decided to retire. Reuters bought Agence Cosmographique from January 1 the following year and now had a clean sweep in French-speaking Europe on which to build profitable French language services. In Germany, Reuters refused to bring in its partner, Vereinigte Wirtschaftsdienste, in which it still had a one-third stake. The computer services were set up as a separate independent company and left VWD in the cold. It was the same story in Italy, Spain, Scandinavia and Holland.

The argument presented by Reuters against its former allies was logical and firm: the agency already had an American partner and the high investment needed, coupled with the low profits, meant there was not enough cake to share round.

As the web of communications spread out from London, a strong hand was needed to deal wtih the telecommunications authorities in individual countries. Many had barely arrived in the age of the telephone before being bounced into the language of satellites and time division multiplexing of voice circuits. The injection of an individual bank's own information into Reuters circuits strained the legal conjuring of what was and what was not permitted on such circuits. It had always been an international rule that no 'third party traffic' could be allowed. If you leased a circuit you could only use it for your own business activities. Reuters had stretched the legal niceties for years when it carried news stories written by correspondents working for its subscribers on its own circuits. Only by moving into this business heavily was the agency able to pay for the costs of reporting the Vietnam war. The legal fiction was preserved by Reuters 'buying' the newspaper's story before transmission and 'selling' it back to the newspaper on delivery. Now the authorities in each country had to be persuaded individually that the new information inserted directly by banks into the Reuters system was also legally acceptable.

Persistent lobbying overcame this hurdle but the real crunch came when Reuters finally unveiled its plans for the electronic market place. These would allow dealers not only to display their prices to each other but even to buy and sell through the Reuters screens, over the wires that Reuters leased. Reuters was not alone in battling to break down the strangleholds imposed by the national telcommunications authorities and finally, in 1981, the Conférence Européenne des Postes et Télécommunications (CEPT) gave the go-ahead for Reuters' dealing service in Western Europe. Two-thirds of the whole company's revenue came from Europe and the signals flashed by the European authorities were quickly accepted by many other countries, though in the case of Japan it took three years before the principle of the Monitor operation was permitted.

By the end of 1981, subscribers from New York, Moscow and across to Peking were able to reach and deal in money with their opposite number in just four seconds, a critical eleven seconds faster than by telephone. The concept of a global electronic market place over a ten-year period had multiplied Reuters' revenue by nearly thirteen times, from £13.8 million to £180 million. The figures for investment in the new leap-frog technology were equally huge. The dealing service cost £8 million to develop, while the company as a whole was investing some £40 million a year in new equipment. Monitor had transformed a struggling news agency into a money-maker.

11

CARVE-UP

'It is extremely unfair to the Newspaper Proprietors' Association to regard them as a lot of greedy bandits.'
—Brendan Bracken, Minister of Information, speaking in the House of Commons debate on the future of Reuters news agency on October 22, 1941.

On May 18, 1983, the Reuters board assembled at the Helmsley Palace Hotel on Madison Avenue. The meeting in New York attracted none of the pomp or publicity of previous gatherings of the agency's top brass on foreign soil. Press interest was the last thing the directors had in mind as they settled into their chairs for what was to prove a critical discussion on the future of the agency.

Top of the agenda was the future financing of Reuters, still a subject of sensitivity. Since Victor Matthews' bombshell seven months before, the Reuters team had managed, with difficulty, to smother rumours that the agency intended to cash in on its millions through a public quotation on the stock market. But events were conspiring to make a decision paramount. The company's annual results were, again, outstandingly good. The revenue from Monitor was flowing in steadily, sending profits soaring 123 per cent from £16 million to £36.5 million. Next year looked even better, with anything up to £50 million being forecast. From the point of view of its Fleet Street shareholders and potential investors alike, Reuters was seen as a company which had hit on a magic formula in a growth market: the computerised transmission and communication of data, better known as information technology.

Those who doubted the wisdom of Reuters going public had to face market facts. The agency's strength lay in its worldwide communications network, reporting and distributing information and data to some 158 different countries. But new alliances were springing up which threatened Reuters' dominance. On its home ground in Britain and in its biggest market, Europe, Reuters' great American news agency rival, Associated Press, had formed an alliance with Dow Jones and the upstart Telerate. The newcomer,

Telerate, only began life in 1969, but when it was floated on Wall Street in 1982 it was valued at nearly $900 million, a phenomenal sum given that its *revenues* only amounted to $52 million. The fact that such ratings were given to companies like Telerate underlined how eager investors were to latch on to the new, glamorous information technology stocks of the future.

The temptation therefore for the board to approve plans for a public flotation of the agency must have been great. Reuters' own executives had refused to be steamrollered into disclosing their position, despite the public cajoling of Victor Matthews the previous October. But Glen Renfrew, the managing director, was by now a convert to the idea of going public. Privately, he was concerned that the agency was in danger of missing a once-and-for-all opportunity to tap the market's goodwill. Though there was no doubt about the company's ability to generate cash, as the growth of 18 per cent, 54 per cent, and 30 per cent between 1980 and 1983 showed, the arguments in favour of the market option appeared overwhelming. Renfrew remembered only too well the painful arguments within the board over borrowing £1 million to fund Monitor at the tail end of the 1960s: was it realistic to expect the company to continue to grow purely out of its own resources? Over the next few years, Reuters would need tens of millions of pounds to stay ahead in the technological race and to fund expansion and possible acquisitions. The problem was how to reconcile this commercial reality with the wishes of the shareholders and the directors, each of whom had very different views both of the agency and on the desirability of going public.

The New York board meeting was the first chance the Reuters board had to discuss the flotation proposals in depth. It was chaired by Sir Denis Hamilton, a brilliant journalist and former editor of *The Sunday Times* who had occupied the Reuters chair since 1979. By 1983, Hamilton was a sick man fighting cancer, but he resolutely attended every board meeting and he was to play an honourable role in holding the ring between the shareholders and the Reuters executives. His own views were less clear: he had sympathy with the agency's financial needs, but he had grave doubts abut turning it into a public company. The strict principles of the 1941 Trust agreement weighed heavily with him.

Hamilton's concern was shared by the Press Association. Until this point, the PA, through its modest chairman, Richard Winfrey, had played a secondary role, leaving the Fleet Street barons to stake their claims and counter-claims. But he was well aware that the barons, though individually fearsome, were collectively weak. By contrast, the PA was a far more unified force and through its 41 per cent shareholding in Reuters it could expect to exert considerable influence in the power-broking to come.

Initially, Winfrey was far from convinced by the arguments advanced in favour of going public.[1] He mistrusted the Fleet Street shareholders and doubted whether their interests in grabbing the money could be reconciled with the need to protect the agency's independence and integrity. He was also irritated by the behaviour of Matthews and Hare, both of whom had declared their hands early in the game.

But Winfrey was a realist. PA's news services were losing up to £2 million a year, proof that making news pay its way in Britain was as difficult as overseas. Until the Reuters dividend in 1982, which amounted to £700,000, PA had to rely on its investment income and this was plainly not enough. In 1982, PA had to sell its joint stake in the jointly owned Extel sports service which was worth £1 million a year. The sale blasted a hole in PA's profits and it was only the Reuters dividend which plugged the gap. To Winfrey, it seemed as if the PA had reached the same position as its sister agency in the 1950s, struggling to make a living and forced to sell off assets to keep its news service going.

Reuters millions could, overnight, transform the fortunes of the PA and its members among the provincial press in Britain, many of whom were battling against a recession in advertising and trade union opposition to new technology. But Winfrey knew that there could be no movement without the agreement of all the shareholders. No amount of public agitation or private pressure could change this.

Inside the Helmsley Palace Hotel conference suite the discussions on Reuters' future drifted back and forth until one shareholder made what Winfrey recalls as the decisive intervention. 'Equity is everything,' exclaimed Rupert Murdoch.

The remark caught everyone off balance. Murdoch had been slouched in his chair, listening to the various contributions and waiting to pounce. After a pause and a mischievous grin, the Australian explained what he meant.

Reuters could issue paper to expand its business. At present it relied on financing growth from its own resources. If it sold shares on the stock market, it could rapidly expand its capital base, which would give it an immediate cash injection. But above all, going public would help future expansion because it gave the agency the flexibility of either borrowing against shareholders' funds or making acquisitions through issuing its own shares. In short, equity was the springboard for Reuters' future growth and development. The board was impressed, and it was agreed to order a study by Reuters' auditors, Binder Hamlyn, of the financial aspects of floating the company on the stock market.

Eight days after the New York board meeting, an unusually well-informed article appeared in the financial pages of the Murdoch-owned *Times* in London. 'Reuters may go public' the headline proclaimed, tentatively.

Murdoch was always one who liked to be first with the news. But this looked suspiciously like a leak through his own newspaper calculated to put pressure on the other Reuters shareholders to agree to float.

Reuters' senior managers were furious. The last thing they wanted was to be bounced into a premature decision on the future of the agency by a mixture of stock market whim and Fleet Street greed. After the sacred Trust had been set up in 1941, successive chief executives, Sir Christopher Chancellor, Tony Cole, Gerald Long and lastly, Glen Renfrew, had run their own show. Reuters was their company, proud and independent. Now, for the first time, it was clear to Reuters' top men, Renfrew, Nelson and Judah, that this independence was an illusion. The agency, in fact, was at the mercy of the shareholders, the very people who had contributed little or nothing to the agency's success. 'Our company, our news agency, our power base was suddenly taken away,' recalled one senior Reuter executive. 'It was a traumatic period.'[2]

On June 10, the day of the annual Reuters board lunch, chairman Hamilton was forced to issue what was intended to be an authoritative denial of *The Times*' story. There was no truth in the rumour that a decision on going public had been made, Hamilton insisted. But several journalists spotted the comic irony in these words. Hamilton was still chairman of Times Newspapers and he appeared to be rubbishing his own newspaper's reporting standards. Moreover, the denial ignored the extraordinary discussions then taking place between Reuters' Fleet Street shareholders at the Newspaper Publishers' Association.

The NPA council chamber is a daunting room. Around a huge oaken table are some twenty green leather chairs, to which each of the national newspaper proprietors can lay claim. If one of the so-called press barons is absent (which is all too often the case), then that chair must lie vacant. The seating arrangement is equally formal: each press proprietor must sit in alphabetical order according to the title or titles of his various newspapers. It is one of Fleet Street's great ironies that the owner of Express Newspapers, the heir of the Beaverbrook tradition, has, under this arrangement, to sit next to his arch rival, Rothermere, the owner of Associated Newspapers, with the Second Viscount Rothermere gazing down on the proceedings from a portrait on the wall.

For several months, the NPA council had at varying intervals discussed Reuters' riches. Victor Matthews' comments about the possibility of turning the agency into a public company had unleashed enormous interest. The problem was how to reconcile the fierce differences of opinion within the council, not only on the desirability of the proposal, but also on just who owned how much of the NPA's 41 per cent stake.

The difficulty arose in the way the Reuters shares were allocated to each individual newspaper. Because the shares were held in trust by the NPA, the individual newspaper groups, such as the Express, the Mail, the Telegraph and Times Newspapers, did not own the Reuters shares directly. They were held, as it were, at one remove. Only by unlocking the Trust could the shares and therefore the Reuters millions flow into Fleet Street's coffers.

As if this were not complex enough, ownership was further confused by an intricate points system under which the NPA's shareholding was split between members: most daily newspapers received six points, a London evening paper three points and a weekly newspaper one point. Fine, except that since these rules had been drawn up in 1941, the pattern of newspaper ownership had changed dramatically. Some newspapers such as the *News Chronicle* and the *Daily Sketch* had folded, while others such as the *Sunday Telegraph* and the *Daily Star* had taken their place. Equally, there was some joint ownership, such as the uneasy co-proprietorship of the *Standard* by Associated Newspapers and Express Newspapers.

The result, in the words of the NPA's chairman Lord Marsh, was a mare's nest of interlocking and disputed shareholdings. Worst of all, there was no proper record of the (now crucial) transfers of shares which had followed the sale or the collapse of various newspaper titles. When the first verbal assaults took place inside the NPA council over individuals' shareholdings, Marsh went down to the NPA's vaults to take a look for himself. He found scraps of paper with inky scrawls suggesting long-lost share transfers, along the lines of 'Fred, I think those Reuters shares belong to you. Yours, Eric'. In the end, Marsh called in the NPA's solicitors Barlow, Lyde Gilbert who spent two weeks searching through the dozens of boxes for Reuters share transfers, while several more weeks were spent reading the minutes of every single NPA council meeting since 1943 to establish the correct shareholding.

The arguments between the individual press barons raged throughout the summer of 1983. Very soon, armies of lawyers, merchant banks and accountants representing the Fleet Street newspapers, were wheeled into the NPA council to check on who might be cheating whom over the shares. Millions of pounds, after all, were at stake; and once the news leaked out that the Reuters board had decided to investigate seriously the idea of going public, the controversy reached a crescendo.

On June 7 the NPA called a meeting which ostensibly should have been to discuss a union dispute at the *Financial Times*. The bad news was there was going to be no *FT* and therefore No Comment on election day on June 9. It was a bitter reminder of the newspaper industry's habit of choosing the critical moment to shoot itself in the foot.

Then Victor Matthews spoke and what followed was the brash press baron's very own front page scoop, enough to turn the *FT* dispute into the equivalent of a two-paragraph filler. Matthews, to the astonishment of all seated around the NPA table, announced that he was close to agreement with Lord Rothermere on the two men's individual shareholding. There was a sigh of relief from those present, for Matthews and Rothermere had been slugging it out toe to toe over their shareholding for weeks, with both men threatening to haul in their lawyers to settle their differences in court.

It was a brief respite, for two days later, at a second NPA meeting, yet another ferocious dispute broke out when Rupert Murdoch revealed with relish that Matthews had not paid his full Reuters subscription when he had launched the *Daily Star*. The Reuters subscription was the one pre-condition to share entitlement. Given that Matthews' stake in Reuters was worth almost £100 million on a valuation of £1 billion, the *Star* shareholding alone was worth between £20 million and £30 million. When the press barons heard the news they almost leapt across the table to strangle the hapless Matthews. And so what appeared to be a long-awaited truce collapsed and the trench warfare resumed.

The early June débâcle was just one of a number of bitterly fought disputes inside the NPA. Others included an attempt by the *Financial Times* to claim a full daily newspaper quota of Reuters shares, but it was soon discovered that the one newspaper in Fleet Street that should have known about such matters financial had, in fact, only signed up as the equivalent of a Sunday newspaper. Other anomalies in the list of shareholders showed the race tipster's guide, the *Sporting Life*, counting as a full daily newspaper, holding six times the interest of the big-selling *Sunday Times*. There was even a half-hearted attempt by the International Thomson Group, former owners of Times Newspapers, to lay claim to Reuters shares. But Rupert Murdoch, having seen *The Times* and *Sunday Times* lose almost £25 million between 1981–2, was in no mood to see his shares wrested away from him and the attack was beaten off. Above all, as one participant recalled, the memorable aspect of the endless wrangles was the sight of the individual proprietors battling it out in person. 'Until then, one had only seen them in their glamorous roles having tea with the Queen or out at a gala. Now, for the first time, one saw men like Murdoch, Rothermere and Matthews in their business roles. They were very fast on their feet, very rough and bloody impressive.'[3]

Behind the rows over individual shareholdings, there were several other more fundamental considerations at stake. To some extent they were tactical: was it in Murdoch's interests to see millions of pounds poured into Matthews' pocket when the *Daily Star* was in direct competition with his best-selling *Sun*? The same applied to Rothermere and Matthews, though in this particular case the personal animosity between the two men was palpable, though Matthews insisted later that Rothermere's opposition was largely due to the fact that he had not thought of the idea of pressing Reuters to go public.[4] And yet there were some NPA members who were far from convinced that it was either right or proper for the Fleet Street shareholders to take the Reuters money and run. The most obvious member of this camp was the owner of the Daily Telegraph Group, Lord Hartwell.

It has been said of Lord Hartwell that he would rather mortgage his own house than see a national newspaper go under. He belongs to the old newspaper school, perhaps the last of the old-style family newspaper proprietors, and at the age of seventy-two he remained implacably opposed to any move which he thought might undermine or threaten Reuters' independence and integrity as an international news agency. As one participant in the fiery NPA council meetings put it: 'Of all the proprietors, it was Hartwell who insisted on preserving Reuters' virginity.'[5]

To some, Hartwell was an obstinate old man standing in the way of a multi-million pound killing. But such a view under-estimates and misinterprets his motives. For he was a trustee of Reuters news agency and as such he regarded himself as a guardian of its principles. He had no intention of allowing any of the hard-nosed tycoons and their representatives in the NPA council to ride roughshod over the Trust until their arguments had been fully debated. Hartwell was to prove a formidable obstacle in the following months to those like Matthews who were determined to cash in their Reuters chips as soon as was decently possible.

Reuters' own management watched the machinations inside the NPA council with a mixture of bemusement and frustration. With journalists now alerted to the story of how Fleet Street had discovered oil at the bottom of its garden, it had become impossible to deny that there was indeed a chance of Reuters going public. On July 14, Glen Renfrew finally disclosed what many had suspected: that the agency had indeed been studying float proposals since the May board meeting in New York. More he could not say, though he might have added that it was impossible to comment while half of his shareholders were at each other's throats over their respective shareholdings in the company.

In the event, it took an outsider to break the deadlock inside the NPA. Peter Gibbings, the self-effacing managing director of the Guardian, proposed a series of meetings in his offices where representatives from the NPA and the PA could both iron out their differences and agree on a feasible plan to turn Reuters into a public company. Gibbings, it will be recalled, enjoyed joint membership of the NPA and the PA through his two newspapers, the *Guardian* and the provincial Manchester *Evening News*, and his position made him a perfect honest broker.

Throughout the summer, Gibbings ran what might be called the equivalent of the Government's Star Chamber, the forum in which departmental Ministers have their public spending plans whittled down by a committee of senior Cabinet Ministers. In this case, Gibbings, aided by Ian Irvine (Fleet Holdings), Alan Hare (the *Financial Times*), Donald Anderson (United Newspapers), Des Anderson (*Herald Weekly*) and J. E. C. Dicks (Joseph Woodhead and Sons) sat in judgment on the various individual newspaper barons' respective claims to Reuters shares, and tried to pare them down.

On one crucial occasion, when everyone began to despair of solving the Matthews-Rothermere dispute, the chairman of Fleet Holdings finally gave way and relinquished a share of the *Standard* to Rothermere, the man who had led the opposition to what he considered to be a sell-out. Gibbings went over to the lugubrious Matthews and said with a trace of irony: 'If I may say so, Victor, that was very magnanimous of you.'

The Rothermere-Matthews compromise settled the outstanding dispute over the respective claims to Reuters shares. But the division of the spoils was if anything simple by comparison with what was to follow. Put simply, the arguments boiled down to three fundamentals: how to ensure that the agency, once it sold shares on the stock market, remained protected against a takeover; how to ensure that such protective devices did not diminish the value of the company and therefore the return to shareholders; and how to reconcile both these aims with the principles of the Reuters Trust, which stated categorically that the agency's independence and integrity had to be upheld.

The most obvious way to protect the agency against predators was to create a new, weighted voting structure so that the present shareholders retained control. In essence, it meant that the owners, through their special shares, would be able to outvote or block any move by new shareholders which threatened the company's independence.

The principle was not unknown. Several major British companies such as Lew Grade's entertainment empire, ACC, relied on special voting rights for certain shareholders to deter outsiders from launching bids. The problem was that the stock market both in London and the United States frowned on such devices: they hindered the free flow of shares, and they weakened shareholders' power to influence the company's management. In London, the big institutional investors, the pension funds and insurance companies, insisted on one share, one vote. Anything less and there was always the chance that they might boycott the issue.

Few Reuters shareholders realised at this stage just how controversial this issue would become. It appeared a technical hitch which could be resolved with some fast sales talk about Reuters as a glamour stock which every cute investor should have in his portfolio. Indeed, in the *Guardian* talks, it was agreed in principle if not in detail that there could be no question of the present shareholders relinquishing control of the company by offering equal voting rights. The Australians were adamant on this point. On several occasions the telephone wires from London to Melbourne went hot as Lyle Turnbull of the Australian Associated Press breathed a fiery opposition to any suggestion of changes in the present ownership, even at the risk of diminishing the value of the company once it went public.

Behind the discussions on weighted voting rights and the ownership of the company the Reuters Trust loomed large. No one was willing to back any proposals which looked as though the shareholders were trampling over the Trust. And yet, the Trust and its strictures on independence formed the main obstacle to cashing in on the company's riches. The shareholders must have felt like the monkey with its fist clasped inside the bottle of sweets: they could feel the goodies, but there appeared to be no way of extracting them. Then Victor Matthews came up with a proposal which appeared to cut through the conundrum.

His suggestion was this: since Reuters' financial services, led by

Monitor, were the real moneyspinners, why not float them off as a separate company? There was, after all, no mention of the financial services in the Trust agreement; so why spend hours devising special protective measures to defend something which was like any other commodity, just a great deal more valuable? There was a typical hardnosed commercial logic to Matthews' argument, and it attracted support from several shareholders. The problem was that it ignored one vital issue: Reuters' news service.

Despite the fact that Reuters' financial services now contributed up to 90 per cent of the company's revenue, the management and staff still saw themselves as working for a news agency. It was an emotional attachment, which affected men like Renfrew and his deputy Michael Nelson as much as the men and women out in the field, whether they were filing stories or selling the latest computerised data base for the Eurobond market. Both Renfrew and Nelson had been journalists before they climbed the executive ladder: Nelson liked to remind colleagues that he too had served as a correspondent in the paddy fields of South-East Asia. To condone any move which appeared to compromise the news service was, in the eyes of Reuters' management, the equivalent of selling one's birthright.

Until this point, their tactics had been to wait until there was unanimous agreement among the shareholders before making their pitch. At a board meeting on September 14 and an informal meeting of key shareholders on September 20, however, they switched to a full-scale assault on any suggestion that the agency should be split between its (profitable) financial services and, by implication, its (unprofitable) news service. Once they revealed their hand, the proposal was swept from the table. The board had already agreed to call in Reuters' financial advisers, the merchant bank S. G. Warburg, to draw up a scheme for floating the company on the stock market which would uphold the principles of the Trust. But Renfrew and Nelson were not satisfied. Just in case there were any lingering doubts, they wrote a four-page memorandum which amounted to a devastating rebuttal of the Matthews plan, as well as a much-needed history lesson on Reuters for the shareholders.[6]

The key passage in the memorandum dealt with the position in which the agency had found itself up to 1973. Until then Reuters had split its business between a General News Division and what it called its Economic Services. The result was a loss-making news service forced to carry the mounting costs of bureaux all over the world, while scraping pennies together selling general news to the world media. The losses, the memo disclosed, were not even covered by a 3 per cent levy on the profitable economic services. And so the news service became the poor relation.

It was the historical problem which Baron Reuter, Roderick Jones, Christopher Chancellor and, in his early years, Gerald Long had faced. The news service had always struggled to pay its way, and no amount of fudging could hide this truth. When, under Tony Cole and Gerald Long, the agency ran the economic and general news with separate staff, separate management and sometimes separate premises, the result was a shambles: 'An inordinate amount of time was spent on arcane discussions on cost allocations between the two divisions. The financial plight of the general news division had a damaging effect on the morale of staff and many journalists resigned during this period. The damage to Reuters of having two chiefs in most centres of the world, who were frequently fighting each other, was considerable.'

Both Nelson and Renfrew had been scarred by this experience and they were determined it should never happen again. And they went on to describe how the management had already taken preventive steps. In the past ten years, the whole thrust of management had been to integrate the two services. This was not just a tactic to cross-subsidise, it was a recognition that it was becoming harder and harder to distinguish the two. In the last resort, Reuters was not merely a news agency but an *information* agency. It was therefore quite wrong to suggest that there was a clear dividing line between the news and financial services; that newspapers, radio and television received the general news, while the businessmen took the stock prices and market data. A journalist filing the latest pork belly price from Chicago adopted the same standards as the reporter sending a dispatch on the latest bomb in Beirut. Both occupations demanded accuracy and they relied on an assumption on the part of the subscriber, business or media, that Reuters and reliability were synonymous. In short, the news service and the financial services were indivisible.

The Renfrew-Nelson memorandum, circulated on September 21, deserves its place in agency history. In the excitement generated by the agency's new-found riches, it was a rare and sober reminder that the price of truth was higher than many of the shareholders imagined.

Indeed, events in Fleet Street soon showed that shareholders' claims that they were mainly interested in the future of Reuters were transparent. On October 13, the paper and publishing empire, Reed International, announced that it planned to float Mirror Group Newspapers on the stock market in 1984, purely on the back of its Reuter stake. Reed had never been happy with its newspaper interests which consisted of six national titles – the *Daily* and *Sunday Mirror*, the *Sunday People*, Scottish *Daily Record*, *Sunday Mail* and the *Sporting Life*. Reed's chairman, Sir Alex Jarratt, found the newspapers 'chaotic' and it was said since Reed inherited the Mirror Group in 1970 when it took over International Publishing Corporation, he had entered the Group's headquarters only once.

It was Reuters – and Mirror Group's 7.8 per cent stake – which gave Reed and Jarratt the chance to pull out. MGN's stake in Reuters was estimated to be worth £78 million and the Reed board thought, falsely as it was to turn out, that its newspaper group could remain independent as a public company.

That week the *Daily Mirror* offered a promise to its readers. 'The sale of the *Daily Mirror* will not weaken our voice nor our independence. We are changing owners but not our policy. The modern *Mirror* has never had a proprietor. That has given us a freedom unknown to other mass circulation newspapers. We want to keep it that way. And a widespread sale of shares to the general public will, we hope, ensure that independence is strengthened.'[7]

It was fantasy. Just nine months later the Mirror Group was snapped up by the publisher Robert Maxwell for £113 million including the Reuters shares. The fate of the *Mirror* was determined indirectly by Reuters, a rude reminder that money was what really mattered.

But at this moment, when the Reuters management appeared to have won the major battle to preserve the agency from its worst enemies, opposition appeared from an unlikely quarter.

On October 22, a three-page article appeared in the *Spectator* magazine under the headline: 'Reuters: The Price of Greed'.

12

CASHING IN

'I could have allowed the agency with its solid corpus and its worldwide reputation to be floated very advantageously as a public company. But, that would have revived the danger: a free market in the shares would have exposed Reuters to the menace of undesirable influence and perhaps control.'
—Sir Roderick Jones, in a letter to *The Times*, October 24, 1941.

The *Spectator* magazine is one of Britain's last surviving periodicals. It was founded in 1828, though it was not the first journal to bear the name. The original *Spectator* was the inspiration of that great man of letters, Joseph Addison, and had enjoyed a brief but interrupted existence between 1711–15. Throughout its history, the *Spectator* has never been afraid of challenging the established view: it backed the Federalists from the outset in the American Civil War, to the fury of its readers; it broke with Gladstone over Irish Home Rule: and, more recently, it strongly opposed Britain's entry into the EEC while its rejoicing at Edward Heath's defeat by Margaret Thatcher was open and unabashed.

Alexander Surtees Chancellor, Eton, Trinity Hall, Cambridge, became editor of the *Spectator* in 1975. Under his guidance the magazine retained an influence which extended way beyond its somewhat precarious circulation of 18,000. It was, in Chancellor's words, a journal with a reputation of stylish outrage. But as he himself admitted, the decision to devote three and a half pages to the question of the future of Reuters was unusual, even by his sometimes quirky editorial standards.

Chancellor's connections with Reuters ran far deeper than he cared to admit in this, his first contribution to the Reuters debate. He joined the agency in 1964, straight after Cambridge, and worked for ten years as a reporter, rising to chief correspondent in Italy between 1968–73. His career fitted neatly into the Gerald Long era, though his own experience had been limited to the reporting of foreign news and not the production and sale of the commercial services. But there were even more powerful reasons why Chancellor chose to deliver his October broadside against the proposed flotation: his father was indeed the former Reuters general manager, Sir Christopher Chancellor. Now seventy-nine and living in a country retreat in Shepton Mallet, Somerset, Chancellor senior had been waiting for some months to make what he hoped might be a decisive intervention in the Reuters drama.

Though the October 22 article appeared under the name of Geoffrey Robertson, a barrister, and Alexander Chancellor, there was no disguising the hand of Sir Christopher in its contents. It began with a withering attack on those who wanted to cash in on the Reuters flotation. The management, said Chancellor junior, had been shifty and the Fleet Street press barons were 'licking their lips in anticipation of the biggest windfall in the history of the British press'. All stood to gain from Reuters going public: the newspaper owners with sums well over £100 million and the senior management who held shares in the agency issued in 1981. Glen Renfrew, the article pointed out, held 545 shares, which – if City estimates of Reuters' £1 billion value were right – would be worth about £10,000 each on the market.

The central purpose of the article was to examine the 1941 Trust and its amended version in 1953 and to question whether or not a flotation was, under the Trust's terms, legal. To be sure, the Reuters management and shareholders had been well aware of the difficulty in squaring the strictures of the Trust with cashing in their shares. But, until the *Spectator* article, the issue had been the subject of private argument rather than public debate. Without exaggeration, it would be fair to say that Chancellor and his co-author Robertson single-handedly ensured that the future of the agency became as controversial a subject as the 1941 rescue by the national press.

Using the experience of Chancellor senior, who had helped draft the original 1941 Trust agreement, and Robertson's knowledge of trust law, the authors were able to probe further into the legality and desirability of the float plan than any other British journalists. As Chancellor pointed out with relish, most if not all of Fleet Street's newspapers had avoided any discussion of any possible legal difficulties since they all stood to gain.

Robertson and Chancellor concentrated on three main issues: the requirement in clause 12 that any attempt to amend or dissolve the Trust must be submitted to and approved by the Lord Chief Justice; and Article 72 of Reuters' articles of association which asserts the duty of the trustees 'to act in accordance with the principles enunciated in the Trust agreement'; and the crucial paragraph one of the Trust which stipulated that the shares be held 'in the nature of a trust rather than as an investment'.

Until the *Spectator* article, few had considered the importance of clause 12 and the role of the Lord Chief Justice. This role had been spelt out by contemporary news reports on the original Trust agreement in 1941; it had also been reiterated by the Royal Commission of the Press 1961–62, when commenting on the proposed sale of the Press Trust of India's sale of its holding in Reuters. 'No other transfer of stock may take place before 1962, and thereafter only with the consent of the Lord Chief Justice . . . After 1962 (but not before), the agreement may be terminated or amended with the consent of the Lord Chief Justice and it terminates in any case twenty-one years after the death of the survivor of certain persons living in 1941.'

There was room for doubt over the precise role of the Lord Chief Justice post-1962. In the eyes of the Reuters management, clause 12 had been the fail-safe device in the 1941 Trust. Drawn up in the deeply uncertain war years, it could be construed as an attempt to call on the authority of an unimpeachable source to prevent the agency being hijacked by its new owners or other predators; but above all it was a device to secure the backing of Parliament to the new ownership arrangement. By invoking the role of the Lord Chief Justice, both Chancellor and Robertson highlighted a fact hitherto overlooked or largely ignored: the importance of the Trust, not merely as an obstacle to change but as a pillar to the agency's credibility.

Nowhere was this more clear than the stipulation that the shareholders should regard their shares as in the nature of a trust rather than an investment. Reuters, the authors pointed out, had boasted about the Trust for more than forty years. It had asked its customers all over the world to believe in it as a guarantee of the agency's impartiality and independence. If the Trust was not legally binding, but merely a well-meaning declaration of pious principles which could give way to expedience, what did that imply for the agency's credibility in the whole of the post-war period?

These were uncomfortable questions for Reuters' management. But the authors had even more pointed questions to pose to the shareholders. In 1982, they had carved up a £1.9 million dividend, and in 1983 it was going to be more than £5 million. If they viewed their holding as an investment to be realised rather than as a trust to be honoured, how did this square with the terms of the 1941 agreement? Furthermore, how could shareholders who doubled as Trustees, such as Lord Rothermere and Lord Matthews, both of whose newspaper groups stood to profit massively from a public flotation, possibly be regarded as dispassionate guardians of the Trust?

Coming in the middle of precarious negotiations between management and the shareholders' committee on the precise terms of the flotation plan, the *Spectator* broadside could not have been better timed or aimed. Michael Nelson and Nigel Judah read the piece, and summoned Alexander Chancellor to lunch at Le Boulestin, the discreet French restaurant near the Covent Garden Opera House.

The sides looked unequally matched. Nelson and Judah, both men who had presided over Reuters' phenomenal turnaround, facing their former cub reporter Chancellor, the man with the bluff Etonian manner, modest to the point of infuriation. The conversation began in a strained fashion. Nelson, particularly, was annoyed about the insinuation that he and other executives had a financial interest in the flotation going ahead. Quite untrue, he said. The executive share scheme was designed as a reward and incentive to the men who had been responsible for the agency's success. No one had presumed that Reuters would go public so soon after the shares had been issued in 1981, and the executives had only come round to the principle of flotation after lengthy discussions. There was no question of the management agreeing to any plan which threatened the agency's future independence or the future viability of the news service.

Chancellor left lunch late that afternoon, still far from convinced and determined to fight what he, and his father, considered to be a point of principle: the integrity of the Reuters Trust.

To his surprise, he found himself an ally, one hidden inside what until then had appeared to outsiders as an impenetrable Reuters camp. Lord Hartwell, the owner of the *Daily Telegraph* and *Sunday Telegraph*, had struggled to halt the stampede towards flotation inside the NPA. Though his newspapers stood to gain by up to £80 million from their stake in Reuters, he had been shocked by the grasping behaviour of his fellow press barons, though there would come a time when even Hartwell could not resist.

At this stage, however, Hartwell was clear in his own mind what needed to be done. Like Chancellor and Chancellor's father, he was an old Etonian. Inevitably, all three found themselves speaking the same language.

The day after the *Spectator* article appeared, Hartwell, still editor in chief of his two newspapers, decided to 'go big' on the Reuters story. The piece contained an interview with Reuters' financial director, Nigel Judah. For the first time, Reuters' management had been smoked out to discuss the Trust and attempt a rebuttal of Chancellor's arguments. Judah suggested that the flotation could be justified by the Trust's fifth objective, namely to ensure that 'no effort shall be spared to expand, develop and adapt the business of Reuters in order to maintain in every event its position as the world's leading news agency'.[1]

Chancellor replied a week later, arguing that if, indeed, the owners of Reuters were to look upon the agency as a source of profit rather than as a Trust then the situation was transformed. 'In the past, their attention has been focused on the Reuters news service and how to maintain its quality at the lowest cost to themselves; if Reuters goes public, their attention will be redirected towards those aspects of the company which are likely to make them money – in other words everything but the news service.'[2]

These were legitimate questions and they demanded answers. Reuters, disturbed by the refusal of Chancellor to heed their executives' arguments that the news service was safe in their hands, reluctantly became drawn into the public debate on the Trust. On October 31, Michael Neale, the official spokesman issued a statement on the role of the Lord Chief Justice. He said the clause requiring reference to the Lord Chief Justice on the sale of shares was incorporated and still applied, but he added, crucially, that the Trust was *not* legally binding.

This view was formally endorsed on November 9 when the board met for five-and-a-half hours to discuss the progress of the flotation plan prepared by S.G. Warburg. There was plenty to chew over on the float proposals and the need for protective devices. Attention then turned to the Trust agreement. It was disclosed that, after extensive legal soundings, the Trust was after all not a Trust *per se*, but a shareholders' agreement. In other words, it could be terminated by the shareholders, providing all agreed. This was, then, the definitive interpretation: it released the shareholders from the obligations that Trusts conferred and, to the satisfaction of all around the table, it appeared to allow everyone to cash in on the Reuters millions.

In the following weeks, the inconsistencies and discrepancies in the Trust agreement, its interpretation, and the role of the Lord Chief Justice were brutally exposed. It was Jim Callaghan, never one to miss an opportunity to play the elder statesman figure, who took the lead, in a letter to the Attorney General, Sir Michael Havers. Callaghan said that the Lord Chief Justice had not been but ought to be consulted over the float according to the principles of the Trust agreement. It was a masterly piece of political opportunism because only ten days before, Lord Lane, contacted by two inquiring *Observer* journalists, had revealed that he had no knowledge of his responsibilities.

On November 10, the day after the Reuters board meeting, Havers' office said that the Attorney General was giving 'urgent consideration' to Callaghan's request for clarification.

Havers, like Lane, was on the spot. The pressure mounted three days later when Christopher Chancellor, by now extremely talkative, told the *Observer* that his understanding was that the Trust was always intended to be legally binding. And to rub the point home, he further disclosed that the then Lord Chief Justice, Lord Goddard, had been involved in drafting the original Trust in 1941, and had been called in to approve changes made to it in 1946 and 1950.

Havers' statement to the House of Commons the following day, that he had no official responsibility in the plans for Reuters to go public, did not alleviate the doubts. The Chancellor-Callaghan camp appeared in the ascendancy. They had shown that the spirit, if not the letter, of the Trust was being breached. On November 4, the chairman of the Reuters Trustees, the crusty Australian Angus McLachlan, issued a statement from Sydney, warning that there was no question of the Trustees 'rubberstamping' the float plan. McLachlan, a former joint managing director of the Australian Associated Press, had been in touch with the Australian shareholders in Reuters for some months and had doubts about the principle of going public. His shot across the agency's bows flashed a reminder to shareholders that the battle was far from over.

The November to December months were black ones for the Reuters management. The public debate irritated them, but above all it revived fears that the agency was about to be exposed to the very political interference which they had spent years resisting and finally escaping in the post-war period. It was the ultimate irony that at the very moment in history when Reuters had become financially secure – and therefore truly independent of government – its future was threatened by politicians.

The danger of interference was well appreciated by the journalists themselves within the agency. They had been neither consulted nor informed about the details of the flotation and, as rumours flew about their company's value and the new ownership structure, they became ever more frustrated. Moreover it was not forgotten that a full year before, just after Victor Matthews first revealed the idea of Reuters going public, they had sent a letter to *The Times* outlining their concern.

Whether through carelessness or a desire not to stir up yet more trouble for Reuters' owners, the letter was never published. It was a strange decision for what was supposed to be a newspaper of record. The letter read as follows:

Dear Sir,

Lord Matthews recently predicted that Reuters shares will be publicly traded. Although the company said it has no plans, Lord Matthews made it clear that some of the owners, influenced no doubt by last year's quadrupled profits of £16m, are trying to bring this about and expect to succeed. Reuters' journalists regard with apprehension any change in the company's long-standing ownership arrangements and the danger, however remote, that control may pass into hands which would undermine the independence and impartiality of Reuter reports.

When independence and objectivity seemed threatened in 1941, a trust arrangement among the owners made the production of objectivity and a reliable news service the company's fundamental purpose. The decision this year to remit profits to the owners for the first time since 1941 established another objective which may conflict with the first. We therefore wish to see the trust arrangements recast in ways which would strengthen the role of the trustees and the method by which they are appointed. The objective should be to give effective voice, independent of the owners, to the interests of subscribers and the general public which is that Reuters should continue to preserve its traditional purpose.

If Reuter shares were to be publicly traded the case for such an arrangement would be overwhelming. Reuters' journalists would be glad to contribute to these objectives.[3]

Of course, no intervention by the journalists at this late stage was likely to undermine the plans to go public. But the fears expressed were understandable. There was an essential cosmopolitanism about Reuters journalists: there were Americans, Australians, French, Filipinos, Indians, Germans, Scots, English and many others inside the agency and most of them had travelled the world. As agency men, used to filing stories where accuracy and speed were primary, they regarded their British newspaper colleagues as engaged mainly in the entertainment business pulling readers with bingo, sex and a bit of violence. It was only now, just as the agency was about to undergo its most dramatic change, that many Reuters journalists realised that these very British newspapers were in fact determining the future of their company.

On December 14 the Reuters board met to consider the final proposals for flotation. There was an air of expectancy at the meeting, for all knew that if there were any last-minute hitches or disagreements there would be little chance of hitting the planned date for flotation in the spring. This was the only possible date during 1984 due to the largest-ever sale of shares planned in the autumn, when the Government intended to sell off 51% of the state-owned telephone company, British Telecom. That evening, a brief press release was issued saying that the board had decided to seek a public flotation of the company and 'to submit a plan to the Reuter trustees for their comments'.

As yet no details were revealed. But the statement told all. If the Trustees were to be asked only for their '*comments*' what real power did they have? On December 16, in a rare public statement to staff, Glen Renfrew attempted to answer this criticism. Having lashed the 'self-appointed guardians of Reuters standards', writing in the press, for innuendo and selective reporting, the agency's managing director turned to the question of the Trust. The preservation of the principles of the Trust, he repeated, had always been paramount, and he was satisfied personally that the plan to be considered by the Trustees contained effective safeguards for these principles. Though the board had received legal advice that the Trust was indeed a shareholders' agreement, this advice did not diminish the 'strong moral obligation' on Trustees, board and management.[4]

Fine words, but they did not obscure the fact that if Renfrew was himself satisfied, there was little chance of the Trustees, for all their supposed moral authority, halting the stampede towards flotation.

It should have been a grand occasion: a House of Commons debate on the future of Reuters, recalling memories of October 22, 1941, when Samuel Storey had attacked, Brendan Bracken defended, and a packed chamber enjoyed the cut and thrust of well-informed discussion. Friday, January 27, 1984, was a pale imitation. When the debate opened, there were only twelve MPs present. They were outnumbered by two to one in the press gallery and three to one by those in the public gallery.

It was the former Prime Minister, James Callaghan, who made the most serious contribution in the course of the five-hour debate. He dismissed the morality of the newspaper owners in their decision to sell Reuters. To discuss that, he said, would be 'as fruitful as discussing the innocence of the train robbers'. The thrust of his argument was that it was Parliament that had pressurised the provincial and the London press to get together during World War Two. It was Parliament that had made the new joint owners bind their undertakings in the form of a Trust agreement. It was to Parliament that the owners should be liable for any changes made in that agreement.

Callaghan's invocation of Parliament's authority with regard to Reuters was an interesting notion, but it misread contemporary history. Parliament had given its blessing to the 1941 Trust, but that was at a time of crisis when the aim was to show that the agency could survive without Government money. In 1984, the agency was flourishing and a new Trust agreement was more likely to be designed to prevent predators attacking Reuters' wealth.

The scheme for flotation presented in confidence to the ten Trustees when they met in London on February 21, contained a number of safeguards to the agency's independence. The proposed restructuring of the company was complex, but it was based on two principles: voting control to remain in the hands of the existing shareholders and the protection of the independence of the news services.

The methods devised by Warburg merchant bank were four classes of shares to be created through the formation of a new public company, Reuters Holdings. The existing newspaper owners would retain control through their 'A' shares, 25 per cent of the equity, where each share would be worth four votes on most matters and subject to limitations on transfer. The 'B' shares, representing 75 per cent of the equity, would be worth only one vote and these shares would be offered to the public. The third class of shares would be reserved for the Reuters executive share incentive scheme, while the fourth was a 'golden share' or 'founder's share' which would have the power to block any concern having more than a 15 per cent stake in the company. Any two Trustees would also have the right to use the golden share, vested within a new company, Reuters Founders Share Company, to prevent any changes which would affect the quality of the world news service or a share build-up.[5]

In addition, the Reuters Trust was to be updated, notably reasserting its duty to supply 'unbiased and reliable news to newspapers, news agencies, broadcasters and other media subscribers and to businesses, governments, institutions and individuals and others with whom Reuters has or may have dealings'. To underline, however, the obvious development of the company from a news agency, the Trust now referred to the need to pay due regard 'to the many interests which it serves in addition to those of the media' and described Reuters as being in *the international news and information* (authors' italics) business'. The new Trust was further strengthened by the newspaper owners agreeing to make a legally binding deed of covenant with Reuters Founders, Reuters Holding and Reuters Ltd. to ensure that its principles were maintained.

The nine Reuters Trustees (the chairman Angus McLachlan was too ill to make the journey to London), were happy to approve the scheme, proclaiming that it represented a considerable improvement on the previous arrangement. The subsequent press reports were favourable: 'Even Chubb locks could not have designed a shareholding structure more burglar proof,' said Lex in the *Financial Times*. Jim Callaghan, too, was full of praise, and Alexander Chancellor writing in the *Spectator* gave it his guarded blessing.

In retrospect, the significance of the amended Trust was that it exposed how flimsy the 1941 document really was. The weaknesses of the Trustees' position have already been touched on: the fact that men like Rothermere and Matthews were compromised by their own newspaper interests as beneficiaries of a flotation; the fact that they were only to submit 'comments' on the float plan; but, above all, the fact that the 1941 Trust was indeed only a shareholders' agreement. As much was admitted by the acting chairman of the Trustees, Geoffrey Upton, of New Zealand Newspapers, after taking legal advice from solicitors Clifford Turner. In other words, the document portrayed as the great declaration of independence in the post-war period was fatally flawed.

Though no one could doubt the sincerity of the campaign fought by Christopher Chancellor, his son and others, they were engaged in a phony war. When the race started to cash in on Reuters' millions, the Trust, as it were, fell at the first fence. For all the fuss over the past two years, this fundamental truth had been spotted by one man in the first House of Commons debate on October 22, 1941. Samuel Storey, then chairman of Reuters, told the House that 'the Trust that is proposed to be set up in this connection has no real powers . . . (and) is revocable'. Six days later, when the Trust was officially established, Storey was forced to resign. Only 42 years later were his words truly vindicated.

In the excitement over the flotation, now seemingly unstoppable after the Trustees' agreement, it was perhaps expecting too much to expose the old Trust to more criticism. Sympathy must, however, go to Renfrew and Nelson. They knew how weak the 1941 Trust was but could not say so for fear of being accused of siding with the shareholders who wanted to cash in. It was an impossible position.

There was a further irony. Having done their best to ensure that the agency was properly protected by a new Trust, new protective voting structures, and a new legally binding agreement between owners and trustees, they now found themselves attacked for engaging in overkill.

The first signs of criticism had come in late January when two of the representative associations of the City of London's biggest institutional investors said they were not prepared to put money in a company with special, favoured voting shares. Both the British Insurance Association and the National Association of Pension Funds were influential voices in the City. The NAPF represented 1,500 members and under normal market conditions could be expected to take a significant stake in a company like Reuters whose growth prospects were glittering and whose track record was exceptional. The problem was that the institutions were fed up with weighted voting within companies. It locked them out of decision-making and generally deprived them of influence. In times past they might have accepted this, but not now. The pension funds alone held £70 billion of funds under their control: it gave them muscle and they were determined to use it.

At the time, the institutional threat was beginning to be taken seriously by Reuters and by Warburgs. It had taken months for Bob Boas at Warburgs to come up with a suitable ownership structure. Having passed the Reuters board and the shareholders he was convinced he could sell it to the City.

By late February Boas had still failed to persuade either the pension funds or the insurance authorities to back down. Nagging doubts began to affect the board. They knew that changing the voting structure was impossible: there would be a public outcry and the newspaper shareholders would never agree. But it began to look as if James Callaghan was right when he remarked on the new Trust: 'I particularly like the legal framework. It will write down the value of Lord Matthews' shares, but I won't weep about that.' It was also likely to dent the hopes of some other, less well-known shareholders who had suddenly entered the scene.

For some months the Press Association had been hunting for 'lost' shareholders in Reuters. In January, the PA launched a national advertising campaign to find the unwitting descendants of the four owners and editors who took up 1,800 shares in the PA when it was set up in 1868 by 120 newspaper proprietors. Because of the PA's shareholding in Reuters, these shares were now worth a fortune. Each 100 shares could be worth £1 million.

Most of the PA shares had been passed on to the respective newspaper companies. But some had failed to do so. As the PA's financial controller, Jack Purdham, explained, there was never any reason for these people to reply to letters because the PA had never paid a dividend. 'We lost track of them about 100 years ago,' he told *The Times* disarmingly.[6]

The largest lost shareholding vanished with the death by alcoholic poisoning of Charles Amesbury Whiteley Dundas, owner of the *Western Daily Telegraph* in Bristol. The last mention of him in the PA files was a letter, dated 1886, in which he was described as a 'gentleman of fortune' who may have been the illegitimate son of the Earl of Zetland. His holding was now worth 1,200 shares.

It was a Wiltshire farmwife, Diana Parsons, forty-four, who was one of the first to get the good news about her Reuters shares. A genealogist telephoned her while she was on a skiing trip in Switzerland with the word that she was probably heir to 1,200 PA shares once owned by her stepfather's grandfather. Her reaction at the time was: 'I mean, I'm not going to go out and buy ten yachts.'[7] That was just as well. Weeks later she learned she had in fact been pushed aside by an unknown stepbrother from her stepfather's previous marriage and at the time of writing, she is contesting the case in court.

Another case involved Charles Preston-Cole, a pillar of London's exclusive Carlton Club, who died in 1956 leaving an estate worth £7. It included, however, 300 PA shares, presumed worthless. Preston-Cole inherited the shares from his common-law wife with whom he had a twenty-year love affair. His PA shares were reckoned to be worth £1.8 million at 1983 prices.[8]

There was a further twist to the shareholding conundrum when, at a meeting of the PA shareholders at the Savoy in February, the new voting structures were explained. Just days before Purdham had had to fly to Dublin to sort out a last-minute tax hitch with the Irish shareholders.[9] The problem centred on capital gains tax. Because the PA, like the NPA, held the Reuters shares on behalf of their members, they could not pass them on without the risk of paying punitive tax. Intense discussions with tax lawyers and then the Inland Revenue had all but resolved the matter, but the Irish suddenly had cold feet. Since they held 12 per cent of the PA and 90 per cent of the votes were needed to support the change in ownership, there was just a chance the motion at the Savoy might fail. In the event, the proposals won total support and Richard Winfrey, the PA chairman, could reflect with some satisfaction that the PA's role in the Reuters story had not degenerated into the infighting apparent within the national newspapers, despite the fact that he had to deal with 120 different members as opposed to a mere twelve within the NPA.

With the PA now fully behind the flotation plan, all efforts switched to selling the company successfully to investors. Warburg's plan was ambitious: the first ever simultaneous flotation of shares in New York and London. Allowing for time differences, the idea was to start trading on Wall Street and then at the last minute move to the London stock market. In retrospect, it might have been too clever. Opposition to the proposed weighted voting structures was growing and at the beginning of April the National Association of Pension Funds put out a 'clear recommendation' that their members should neither underwrite nor subscribe to the issue.[10]

It appeared to be a pompous, bloodyminded move by men who had little understanding of the news agency or the need for special measures to ensure that it remained independent.

But there were shareholders, notably Rupert Murdoch, who argued strongly against weighted voting shares. He regarded them as a typical piece of British hypocrisy: the shareholders wanted to cash in on their shares while simultaneously retaining control of a company to which they had contributed next to nothing. However, Ian Fraser, emerging from the shadows, wrote to the *Financial Times* on May 10 and argued that the opposition to weighted shares was misplaced:

> The proprietors and managers of Reuters are absolutely correct in their decision that this integrity and independence must be maintained by belt and braces. Throughout its history, Reuters has been intermittently threatened by the attempts of politically ambitious persons and governments to secure control of (this) unparalleled source of information with a view to subverting the information into propaganda for their own purposes. There is no lack around the world of such potential threats today.
>
> The purpose of the belt and braces protection is not, I repeat not, to perpetuate the tenure of management. Reuters' management will still be able to be sacked at any time by the original newspaper publisher shareholders in the UK and Australasia. Nor is it designed to guarantee control to an ever-diminishing and ever-less-involved family proprietorship. These two features accompany most differential voting systems, and the institutions are right to oppose them.
>
> Reuters is quite different. The issue here is freedom of information and the temptation which a unique instrument such as Reuters would offer to those who would like to corrupt it.

Despite Fraser's defence of weighted voting, the effect was to dampen expectations from the float and to put yet more pressure on Reuters' management to sell hard to overcome the boycott. This in turn created problems across the Atlantic, where an ever-vigilant Securities and Exchange Commission was watching for any evidence of pre-sale publicity.

When Renfrew, Nelson and Judah set off on May 20 for a gruelling programme of promotional roadshows in Boston, New York, Chicago, Minneapolis, Los Angeles and San Francisco, they knew they were in for a hiding to nothing. Share prices had collapsed on both sides of the Atlantic after a wave of speculation about an international banking crisis and fears of higher interest rates. These had been triggered by the bail-out of the Chicago-based Continental Illinois bank, but there were wild rumours of other major US banks, notably Manufacturers Hanover, being in trouble.

Renfrew could point to 1983 profits up from £36 million to £55 million. But as one big US investment fund manager remarked after Reuters' presentation in Chicago: 'They seemed scared stiff when questioned about their sales growth.' Others complained about the team's 'machine gun' approach where facts and figures shot out in an all too brief ninety minutes. Naturally, some of the Americans were playing hard to get but, all in all, everyone seemed, in the words of one manager at Lazard Frères, 'mesmerised by the market'.

These remarks, reported on the front page of the *Financial Times* on May 29, were certainly damaging to the float prospects. The *FT* reporter concerned, Clive Wolman, had followed the Reuters men on the American tour doggedly; when he was barred from the Chicago presentation, he 'doorstepped' the meeting and grabbed as many fund managers as possible for their comments. He then tied these unflattering remarks to a suggestion in his article that Reuters had been ticked off by the Securities and Exchange Commission for offering too much publicity before the float. Renfrew, Nelson and Judah were furious: they accused Wolman of writing an article out of pique, and complained bitterly afterwards that of all the articles written about the company in the two-year build-up to going public, Wolman's was the most disgraceful piece of reporting they had encountered.[11]

Warburgs and Rothschilds, the two advisers to Reuters and the PA, had put a value of between £708 million to £920 million on the company. If that seemed way below the previous £1 billion to £1.5 billion estimates of a year before, there were good reasons for the scale down. The weighted voting shares, the threatened institutional boycott and the fact that the weighted 'A' shares amounted to a quarter of the company's capital, all reduced the pot of gold. In turn, it also reduced the sum which the various newspaper groups could expect to pick up once the agency became a public company. Indeed, Rupert Murdoch, canny as ever, was the sole Fleet Street shareholder who refused to cash in any of his Reuters shares.

Murdoch had been bitterly critical of Warburgs' caution on the striking price for the shares at a meeting on the Sunday before flotation. He, like other major shareholders such as Victor

146

Matthews, had regarded 200p as a minimum, with hopes of 220p when the offer was launched on May 16. In the event, the price was set at 196p, which netted sellers of shares a mere £209 million. Reuters itself picked up £50 million. In addition to the disappointment over the price, the New York float was by no means a clear success. Reuters' New York advisers, Merrill Lynch and Morgan Stanley, managed to find underwriters for only 49 million shares compared to the 39 million shares on offer. It did not escape the newspapers owners' attention that the entire issue of 106.8 million shares could have been handled in London where a late surge of interest meant that the issue was 270 per cent oversubscribed.

After all the anguish and argument over the terms of the float and the future of the agency, the events of June 5 appeared very much an anti-climax. Renfrew, asked if he was happy with the price, said: 'There is no point in being happy or otherwise.' Amid the recrimination, it escaped almost everyone's attention that a predator had slipped into the market to snap up 12 per cent of Reuters 'B' shares, just three per cent below the agreed limit for any single shareholder. The buying had been conducted secretly through nominee companies and must have been planned with extraordinary care so as not to alert the rest of the market. Two days after the flotation, with the price barely at a premium, the anonymous buyer revealed his identity: the Abu Dhabi Investment Authority.

The fact that the Arabs had bought a stake in the world's most famous news agency was barely remarked upon in the British press. For the Reuters management, the raid was the clearest indication yet that going public really did herald a new era in the agency's history.

13

AFLOAT

'The incorruptibility of Reuters' news network is an inherent part of Reuters' success.'.
– Ian Fraser, Chairman of Lazards's in a letter to the *Financial Times*, May 10, 1984.

News agencies will often send out eye-catching, off-beat stories on the wire, but the UPI despatch on May 4, 1985 was what American copy editors call 'a zinger'.

The author was a UPI investigative reporter, Gregory Gordon; his story gave the world the first authoritative account of how Gordon's own news agency had been wrecked — by its owners. One week earlier, UPI had sought protection from its creditors under Chapter 11 of US bankruptcy proceedings, claiming $45m in liabilities.

Gordon's lead read: 'United Press's chief owners reneged on a pledge to invest $2m in the wire service and channelled millions of dollars of scarce company funds into questionable venture deals, present and former UPI officials say. . . Ruhe and Geissler also paid $2.3m to their own management company and hundreds of thousands of dollars to consultants who provided no useful products.'[1]

Douglas F. Ruhe and William E. Geissler were not the most obvious candidates to run an international news agency. They were two former political activists and adherents of the Baha'i faith who owned a firm called Focus Communications, whose chief asset was a struggling television station in Joiliet, Illinois. The two men were virtually unknown outside their business base in Nashville, Tennessee. The story of how they bought the news agency and how in four helter-skelter years they brought it to its knees, provides a lesson to all those who felt squeamish about the newly-found profitability of one of UPI's arch rivals, Reuters.

United Press, founded in 1907 by Edward Wyllis Scripps, a maverick Mid-West publisher, once ranked among the top international news agencies, alongside Reuters and Associated Press. At its peak in the early 1960s, when it merged with Hearst's faltering International News Services to become UPI, the American agency had nearly 6,000 domestic clients, including more than 1,000 newspapers. But faced with a steady decline in the number of US dailies, and with stiff competition from other news services, UPI began to lose both money and clients. By June 1982, it was leaking losses of around $1m a month.

UPI's parent, the E. W. Scripps company had toyed with selling the news agency as far back as 1978. Scripps executives tried to persuade American news organisations to form a consortium to support UPI, along the lines of the established publishers' cooperative which had successfully run the Associated Press. The AP model had worked because AP could simply bill its members for expenses; UPI, by contrast, had clients, not members, and any losses had to be met out of its own pocket.

About two-thirds of the three dozen news organisations pledged support, but some of the biggest players – The New York Times Company, Knight-Ridder Newspapers and The Times-Mirror Company – stayed on the sidelines, saying they could not persuade their shareholders to invest in an ailing business. Scripps tried again, setting up a meeting in New York with some of America's biggest publishers. But loyalties and emotional ties counted for little. As one former UPI president Roderick W. Beaton, explaining Scripps' subsequent decision to put the new agency up for sale, put it: 'If I were a Scripps, I'd have to say to myself, why am I the sucker. Why am I the mule being kicked?'.

In 1981, Reuters took a look at UPI's books. In theory a purchase had its attractions: Reuters could knock out one of its major, if struggling, competitors. But after on-off negotiations lasting a year, Reuters backed away. As one Reuters executive familiar with the UPI talks put it: 'On the outside, UPI looked OK, but once you started peeling off the wallpaper and looked underneath, it was a very different story.'

Around the same time, Ruhe made his first approach to Scripps executives. He and Geissler had barely got their Joiliet television station on the air, but their idea was to set up a mini-network of TV stations and some small broadcast and news organisations. The drawback was that neither Ruhe nor Geissler had any experience in the news wire business.

At first, the Nashville double-act was given the brush-off. But by February 1982, Scripps was ready to consider a forced sale. The details have yet to be fully revealed, but according to a well-documented account published in the *Columbia Journalism Review* in September 1985 by Katherine Seelye, an editor of *The Philadelphia Inquirer* and Lawrence Roberts, a freelance writer and former UPI bureau chief in Madrid, Ruhe and Geissler's second approach came within days of the collapse of the Reuters negotiations. So eager were Scripps to hand over the news agency, wrote Seelye and Roberts, that they topped up UPI's underfunded pension fund, threw in an estimated $900,000 in lieu of certain tax credits which the new owners could not claim and even paid off a $100,000 fee owed by Geissler and Ruhe to their financial advisers, Bankers Trust. In the last resort, the new owners 'did not hand over even a symbolic dollar bill'.[2]

Under Geissler and Ruhe's stewardship, UPI embarked on a helter-skelter ride which saw reckless expansion and contraction mixed with a series of questionable business deals which confounded the company's 1,600 domestic and foreign employees. Both men subsequently denied impropriety and pointed out, correctly, that UPI was in severe financial trouble when they took over the company. But UPI reporter Gordon's story exposed how Geissler and Ruhe had compounded the news agency's difficulties by setting up a series of loss-making subsidiaries with interests, such as real estate, which were tangential to the main business of providing the world with a quality news service.

By September 1984, when UPI employees were asked to take a 25% wage cut, the notion that Geissler and Ruhe were mismanaging the company was pervasive. Foreign correspondents found their telephones temporarily cut off because of non payment of bills, while other reporters were not being reimbursed for hotel and travel expenses.

The marked contrast in the fortunes of UPI and Reuters had been highlighted, just four months before, when UPI sold its prestigious foreign news picture service to Reuters (which had no picture service of its own) for $5.76m. UPI executives said the price was way below market value but as Ruhe admitted to his own reporter Gordon: 'If we hadn't desperately needed the cash, we wouldn't have done the Reuters deal.'

In the months that followed, Ruhe and Geissler found themselves caught in a cash-crunch which tax avoidance, asset sales and wage cuts could not break. In March 1985, one of UPI's main creditors, Foothill Capital, forced the two men to step aside and Luis Nogales, an executive vice president originally hired by Ruhe and Geissler, took over. In June, with no prospect of meeting UPI's liabilities, Nogales sought protection from creditors.

Under Chapter 11 proceedings, UPI was allowed to continue its operations on the grounds that management was to reorganise the company. So the news agency wire service continued to function, as dramatically illustrated by the Gordon despatch documenting the news agency's collapse. Aside from the wheeler-dealing and the intrigue, there was a wider point about the UPI story: there was nothing sacrosanct about a news agency losing money.

As Glen Renfrew said prophetically in 1981 when he took over as chief executive of Reuters: 'Substantial rising profits are the only guarantee that we shall be able to defend ourselves and prosper.'

On May 10, 1985, Reuters celebrated its first year as a public company since the turbulent reign of Roderick Jones. That day, the value of the news agency stood at more than one and a half billion pounds. Reuters' shares had come within a penny of doubling since the flotation the previous year; profits for 1984, at just over £74 million before tax, were only just short of the company's entire turnover five years before. Sir Denis Hamilton, in the Reuters chair for the last time, could expect few complaints from shareholders whose numbers had swelled beyond the confines of newspaper owners to some 17,000 individuals, ranging from the big pension funds to the average stock market punter.

In Fleet Street, the effect of Reuters' wealth had already been felt. All newspaper owners, apart from Rupert Murdoch, had sold a chunk of their shares on the open market in July, realising up to £20m apiece. Indirectly, the value of each national newspaper group's shareholding was more significant because it provided an unrealised asset against which the groups could borrow money from the banks to finance their plans to finally break loose from Fleet Street.

Soon after the public flotation, several groups announced plans to invest tens of millions of pounds in new technology to print their mass circulation newspapers. At first, it looked like old news dressed up to give the impression of change. But this time there appeared a genuine collective will on the part of the owners to make the break. The *Daily Telegraph*, the *Guardian*, Lord Rothermere's Associated Newspapers, and Rupert Murdoch's News International all set out plans for moving into modern printing plant in London's docklands and negotiations opened up with the print unions.

Lord Hartwell, once wary of joining the stampede to cash in on Reuters millions, unveiled plans to raise £110m from City investors and the banks. No more the grimy, dark machine room in Fleet Street where 14 rotary presses each spewed out 14,000 pages an hour for the *Daily Telegraph*; the future lay down the Thames in the Isle of Dogs where four new Goss Headliner Presses, in light and airy surroundings, would have a speed of 60,000 pages an hour. Reuters shares provided the catalyst for the move, though sharp-witted analysts noted that of the £110m, some £38m would go towards redundancy payments, a legacy of years of overmanning in the printing and distribution of Britain's top-selling quality daily.

Elsewhere, the value of Reuters shares inside the national newspapers made them a far more attractive investment – or takeover target. An ambitious 49 year-old merchant banker David Stevens, who also doubled as the chairman of United Newspapers, publishers of *Punch*, the *Yorkshire Post* and several valuable American technical magazines, launched a £280m bid for Matthews' Fleet Holdings. The *Telegraph's* efforts to attract City of London funding caught the attention of a free-wheeling Canadian businessman, Conrad Black. Inside two hectic weeks, Black was on the *Telegraph* board with a 14% shareholding in the group, well poised for a takeover if Hartwell and the Berry family showed a desire to relinquish control.

At the bottom end of the market, the catalytic effect of the Reuters shares on newspaper groups' balance sheets also spurred change, though here the threat of Eddie Shah, the strike-breaker from the provinces, was ultimately more significant. Shah, who had taken on and beaten the powerful National Graphical Association print union at his Stockport newspaper, unveiled plans to produce a national daily, equipped with colour, and employing just 700 workers. Since most of Shah's competitors – Murdoch, Rothermere, Matthews and Robert Maxwell's Mirror Group were labouring with workforces at least three times that size – the threat was real. Maxwell told his 4,500 London workers in August 1985 that if they were not prepared to be guided towards new technology by the rudder, they would be 'taught by the rocks'.

Bold words, which were tempered soon afterwards when Maxwell called off his threat to pull out from Fleet Street and confined withdrawal to his racing paper, the *Sporting Life*. Such semi-victories appear to vindicate the judgment of *Observer* columnist Michael Davie who noted: 'The absurd, age-old Fleet Street battles will go on, funded by the Reuters carve-up but fought with weapons, slanted news, hyped-up news, non-news – that Reuters has traditionally regarded as beneath contempt.'

Outside the narrow confines of Fleet Street, the impact of the Reuters flotation was even more marked. The news agency, already financially strong and richer by more than £50m in cash from the sale of a chunk of its shares, was ready to make the acquisitions which could make it an even more powerful presence in the global financial information business.

In May 1985, Reuters offered $35m for a 20% stake in Institutional Networks Corporation (Instinet), an American company, which provided an automated trading service allowing subscribers to bypass the stock exchange and execute buy and sell orders directly. The deal included an option to buy another 31% and therefore control of the company. But the acquisition brought Reuters into conflict with a British institution which, much like Fleet Street, had failed to adapt to change: the London Stock Exchange.

Reuters had never enjoyed the close relationship with the Exchange that outsiders might have imagined. Back in 1872, a separate company, the Exchange Telegraph (Extel) was founded with the express aim of reporting stock prices and dividends; very soon it obtained exclusive rights to report the London market. Reuters was left flat-footed since, in reporting this market to the world, it was forced to get each price second-hand from Extel.

As soon as computers arrived, Reuters persuaded most of the important European stock exchanges to allow a leak of their original price information into the Reuters system. Where exchanges did not have their own system, they allowed Reuters operators to key in prices as they were traded so the agency could send them to subscribers around the world. Only London resisted this change. Reuters was not allowed to quote 'real time' prices: if subscribers wanted an instant price, they had to contact the market direct.

Reuters had no problem with other London markets. The agency's reporting equipment went into the rubber, cocoa, sugar and coffee markets, while Reuters' price report from the London Metals Exchange had for many years set an international standard for buying and selling copper, tin, lead or zinc. By 1985, however, in a dramatic illustration of the company's new-found strength and confidence, Reuters was ready to mount its challenge against Throgmorton Street.

The London Stock Exchange, for all its avowed success in pulling in business, both international and British, was until very recently a cosy club. Its members regulated their own affairs and worked within a system where charges for conducting trading – the so-called commissions – were fixed according to minimum rates. Central to this structure was the division between the broker – who quotes stock prices – and the jobber, who executes the deal.

By the early 1980s, the system was beginning to break down as investors and competing foreign securities firms took advantage of the internationalisation of financial markets to take business away from London. In 1983, the Conservative government, recognising the need to preserve the London market's competitiveness, agreed to drop a pending Restrictive Practices case against the Stock Exchange in return for a commitment from the Exchange to scrap minimum commissions within three years.

Big broking houses, gearing up for the 'Big Bang' – the date when fixed commissions would go – immediately set up new partnerships with the capital-rich British merchant banks. Foreign banks and brokers, anxious not to be left out, struck marriages with the remaining stockbrokers and jobbers; and, amid the feverish match-making, a vicious brawl began to capture the talent and skills deemed necessary to survive in the new deregulated market.

On top of this internal upheaval, the Stock Exchange, led by its wiry chairman Sir Nicholas Goodison, found itself fighting on a second front. Reuters' Instinet deal threatened to render the Stock Exchange's own trading mechanism redundant.

Goodison and his members had already spent several million pounds on the Stock Exchange's own 'Topic' system to report prices. The system provided some 3,000 terminals in the City of London, and the Exchange was committed to spending at least another £5 million to bring in a refined service which would match the needs of the deregulated market: the Stock Exchange Automated Quotation System (SEAQ).

Outwardly, the Stock Exchange was confident. 'We are more than a match for the Reuters of this world', said George Hayter, director of information services. But, privately, many members thought differently. They could see that even the planned SEAQ system could ultimately become the trading floor thus rendering the Stock Exchange's own, physical trading floor at Throgmorton Street obsolete. Others went further, arguing that if prices were going to be matched on computer, why not go for Reuters' American system which was already in operation?

Glen Renfrew hid his natural Australian bluntness when asked what Reuters' intentions were: 'Our strategy is to be the international link between *established* (authors' italics) methods of exchange.' But many experts reckoned that, ultimately, Reuters had to be the global exchange: the market place with price data from all the world's major markets and the system for buyers and sellers to trade. The global trading floor, working around the clock with Reuters at its centre, was, in their view, just around the corner.

These were heady prospects, but they had to be set against the threat of international competition equally aware of the profits to be made in the financial information business. As Walter Wriston, chairman of the world's biggest bank, Citicorp (known in the UK as Citibank), warned his banking competitors in October 1983: 'We will see a whole new group of companies aiming at our market . . . Information about money has become almost as money itself, as evidenced by the explosive growth in electronic banking. It does not take any leap in the imagination to see that the Reuters, the Dun and Bradstreets, and the Dow Jones with their terminals in our banks and in our customers' back offices now have everything they need to look like a bank except a clearing mechanism.' Two years later, following his nose, Wriston accepted an invitation to join the Reuters' board.

In London, apart from the Stock Exchange, at least a dozen organisations offered prices from the stock and commodity markets. Some of these were run by the markets themselves and some by brokers or independent providers of information. Such was the flexibility of the technology now available that Reuters, like the Stock Exchange, could not expect to control precisely the activities of competitors, even if it so desired.

In Western Europe competition came in some cases from erstwhile news agency allies such as VWD in West Germany, where Reuters had disposed of its one third stake in 1981 and the German agency had tied up with both Quotron and Telerate. The Swiss banks had banded together to get their information direct from the United States via their own leased transatlantic data circuit.

But it was in the United States that the battle had yet to be fought and won. Reuters' representatives had been there since the earliest news agency days; their own man had hired a tug to overtake the mailboat out of New York with the news of the assassination of President Lincoln and scooped the opposition into London by two days.

Reuters' problem was that the American market was largely self-sufficient. Domestic news and prices were always more important than those from overseas. Reuters' managers had to struggle against a prejudice of things not American – even the name of Reuters was mistaken for a brand of German soap. For years, therefore, the British-based agency had lagged behind the American quote vendors, while its commercial news had to compete with the established and extensive coverage offered by the *Wall Street Journal* and Dow Jones' coast-to-coast teleprinter service.

In 1967, Associated Press, under its forceful general manager Wes Gallagher, had broken the 'news swap' arrangement with Reuters which allowed the two agencies' general news services to be exchanged without payment on either side. Under the original deal, which dated back to 1893, the AP had paid a fee to Reuters which reflected the premium that both attached to the Reuter service. Under Roderick Jones, Reuters was forced to concede parity, but Gallagher demanded that Reuters pay a premium of $100,000 for the American service. 'We are not prepared to swap an elephant for a mouse', Gallagher told Gerald Long who promptly accepted the challenge and set Reuters on course for nose-to-nose competition with the Americans.[3]

By July 1985, there were signs that Reuters was to face a renewed bout of competition with the Americans. Dow Jones, through the British money brokers Exco, bought control of Reuters' information rival, Telerate, which had some 11,000 terminals in the United States and Canada. Reuters, meanwhile, had already made a significant move three months earlier by buying Rich Incorporated, an American firm which was the leading manufacturer of computer equipment and programmes for financial trading rooms. The price of $60m was not huge by the standards that now applied but the prize was much larger: at a stroke, Reuters had bought inside knowledge about the design, equipment and operation of every trading room in North America.

A second deal offered further clues on where Reuters managers saw the future course of the business. In August 1985, Reuters agreed to take control of Visnews, the London-based newsfilm cooperative with 400 cameramen around the world and a film library which dated back to 1896, including the old Gaumont Graphic, Empire News bulletins and British Paramount.

Ownership of Visnews was divided into one third stakes between the British Broadcasting Corporation, its equivalents in Canada, Australia and New Zealand, and Reuters. Like Reuters, Visnews enjoyed a constitution and Trust agreement to protect its independence. Similarly, it had expanded despite the limited ambitions of its owners, coupling a lively and growing corporate communications business with a steady income from its film archive, a favourite with the American television networks.

Under the deal, the Visnews shareholding was to be rearranged with Reuters taking a 55% controlling stake while leaving the BBC and its three Commonwealth partners each with 11¼%. The logic lay in building up still further Reuters' communications network. The purchase of UPI's picture service the previous year had already added one dimension (even if that venture was not making money) and Reuters now had five key business areas: textual news for media and commercial subscribers; price and information retrieval, a dealing service based on the original Monitor concept;

news pictures; and finally television news film. Coupled with Reuters international subscriber network and a growing database, this integrated communications business looked more than a match for any competitor.

Inevitably, these deals served to underline the transformation of Reuters from a news agency to an information technology hybrid. They served also to dampen the passions raised during the flotation debate, a debate often clouded by emotive questions: why should the newspaper owners as absentee landlords benefit from an enterprise to which they had contributed so little? How was it possible to side with men who had exposed the weakness of the wartime Trust which had undermined the ideals of many who had worked for and promoted its concept for the succeeding 40 years?

The original Trust had been set up to preserve the integrity of the Reuters news service and the owners had admitted that it was not enforceable. At best it was an undertaking of honour. In its place, the owners proposed a Trust company which would have genuine legal powers even though it could only operate in a defensive capacity. On the surface, the new agreement appeared burglarproof, but others in the newspaper world were more cynical. They had seen Rupert Murdoch drive a coach and horses through the supposed cast-iron guarantees approved by Parliament when he took over Times Newspapers.

The 1941 Trust survived because people believed in it and wanted it to work. It was set up to protect Reuters from the Government and its owners from each other. The agency's new found wealth did not mean that the British Government relaxed its attempts to control the flow of news from time to time. At the height of the Falklands War, the head of the 'D' notice committee – the Whitehall committee which has the power to see that the British media does not publish anything which it considers detrimental to the national interest – rang Reuters and demanded to speak to the editor of its world services.

The official told the editor that he had seen a story about the liner Canberra steaming around in circles off Ascension Island. 'You know perfectly well that ship is full of British troops', he fumed, 'It's an ideal target for the Argentines if they get to hear of its position. Where's your sense of patriotism, man?'.

The editor was a little upset. 'Well, I don't see what that has to do with me', he replied. 'I'm German.'[4]

In every international conflict Reuters had aimed, usually successfully, to have correspondents on both sides. Even the British government at times recognised Reuters' neutrality: it deliberately cut out Reuters in the first schedule of foreign correspondents assigned to cover the Falklands war in its attempt to ensure strictly partisan reporting.

Reuter's independent line meant selling commercial services to communist countries at the height of the Cold War. When the Americans imposed a ban on trade with Cuba after the missile crisis, Reuters sent key price information to Havana via Canada to help keep the Cuban sugar industry going. Communist countries and rightwing dictatorships alike continued to receive and pay for Reuters' commercial services even though they occasionally kicked out their correspondents. The argument, clearly recognised by Gerald Long and his successors at the top of Reuters, was that financial muscle was one of the essential elements to avoid being pushed around by the British – or any other foreign government.

As the new publicly-owned, privately controlled Reuters digested its first year, some still asked if there was any danger that the company might devote less money to reporting general news for the media. On the surface such doubts seemed pointless: the number of journalists employed and the number of Reuters' offices had both grown by 20% over the previous five years. But, the critics went on, there would inevitably come the day when profits dropped instead of continuing to rise at a meteoric rate. They pointed to the company's dependence on the Monitor system and the dangers of it being outdated. In 1984 the money services of Monitor alone produced 66% of Reuters' revenue. Information about commodities supplied 18%, and about securities 11% of revenue.

The entire income from media services, once the flagship, totalled just 5% of Reuters' revenue. There was always the risk that international currency rates might one day stabilise and the lesson there was simple: no price movement meant no news, and that spelled no business. The fixed costs of running and distributing and instant information system with all the necessary back-up were huge. Once these costs had been covered the profits could be vast but, if the number of subscribers dropped below a certain level, the losses could also be horrendous. The Monitor system itself was nearly ten years old and its original versatility was now in question.

On the question of Monitor, Reuters could point to the recall of Patrick Mannix, the original architect of its technology who was assigned the express brief to replace the whole network by 1988. By then, Reuters promised, it would cover the sort of requirements that customers today had not even considered. It would take in new developments in artificial intelligence, largescale data storage, information privacy and it would move to 'one stick control' of mixed data from various suppliers. It was impossible to forecast exactly what information would be needed in the years ahead. But, Reuters insisted, the demand for fast information would increase, and its own enhanced and super-versatile network of communications would cope with it.

Nevertheless, doubts persisted. The first protective Reuters Trust had spoken grandly of ensuring that Reuters produced the best possible international news service. But the costs of keeping just one working correspondent overseas were, 45 years on, phenomenal. Shareholders could point to several dozen places where a full-time employee's labours might result in a few column inches a month in isolated newspapers across the world.

Both directors and top management had a consistent reply: prices and news were indivisible. This missed the main point: the company could operate at the same level with its commercial services and still cut back a large number of correspondents and offices that were not strictly necessary to the newsfile. Such places had been covered by part-time correspondents for most of Reuters' history and no doubt this could happen again.

Against this, many countries related their international news standing to the size of the Reuters presence. If Reuters had no correspondent of its own to report such countries to the world, there was always the risk that the commercial services could meet difficulties in operating there. Such blackmail from Third World or non-democratic regimes might appear crude, but there was no doubting the publicity value that a resident Reuters correspondent could provide.

Despite a seemingly prosperous future there were inevitably those who asked what would happen if at some time Reuters simply could not afford to sustain the sort of news service that the new protective Trust guaranteed. Was it possible that the successors to Sir Roderick Jones would, one day like him, go cap in hand to the British Government for help? They could point to the British Broadcasting Corporation which, despite incessant political and financial wrangling, continued to operate with an international reputation for objectivity although its funds came partly from government grants and partly from licence fees that the government approved.

On the other side of the Channel, the French News agency, Agence France Presse, continues to operate around the world and its services are taken and used by such newspapers as *The Times* in London.

It is no secret that the budget of AFP contains each year some 60% of Government money. The published budget turnover for 1984 at 630 million francs (£55 million) included a state subsidy of

394 million francs (£35 million). AFP is the direct successor of the original French agency, Havas, and can therefore trace its origins back even further than Reuters. Despite its Government connections, the AFP service is still treated with respect by independent editors whose only doubt is that it can remain objective on key national issues at a time of French crisis. Such editors assume they can spot those occasions and are sufficiently alert not to be taken in.

Despite the success of AFP and the French government's apparent satisfaction with its financial control of the prime source of both national and international news, it is virtually impossible that the British Government would contemplate any financial rescue for Reuters. Past experience alone would make it unthinkable. In any case, control of the national broadcast television and radio services would be more effective in an emergency. The BBC, despite its guarantees, was within two days of being taken over during the 1956 Suez crisis and the Government had, by that time, already taken over and was operating their subsidiary regional transmitter, Sharq-al-Adna, in Cyprus.[5]

In the last resort, the independence and the integrity of the new Reuters and its services is not going to be protected for the future by locking in as majority shareholders, arbiters of its accuracy and guardians against takeover, a group of newspaper owners whose business interests are no longer in parallel with Reuters. The successors to those who constructed the wartime Reuters Trust may have built a stronger safe but they have not thrown away the key. Sooner or later they will disappear and the question of the Trust will arise again.

In the public eye, and far too often in the eyes of the British press, Reuters is still a news agency, albeit now a prosperous one. Since the dark days of 1941, the news market has been overtaken by technology. News itself is seen to happen through the eye of the camera and less through the eyes of a correspondent. Newspapers, with notable exceptions, have moved increasingly towards vehicles of entertainment and away from being prime sources of news. This is what makes Reuters so valuable, and so unique. Reuters has the opportunity to build on its exacting tradition of accurate reporting providing it has the money to do so, as dramatically illustrated by the demise of UPI. The media tip of Reuters is the exposed part of a highly sophisticated and complex information business that has to be accurate, second by second, every day of the year. If it is not accurate it will not sell its products.

Any owner that tampered with the facts today would very quickly have no business left to run.

Appendix 1

THE SELLING

SHAREHOLDERS IN REUTERS

Name	Prior to Combined Offering		Number of B Shares to be sold in the Combined Offering	After Combined Offering*	
	Number of B Shares Owned	Percent of Class**		Number of B Shares Owned	Percent of Class**
Associated Newspapers Holdings plc[1] [2]	27,383,452	10.5	8,787,578	18,595,874	6.6
Associated Newspapers Group plc[2]	1,893,826	0.7	1,368,711	525,115	0.2
BPM Holdings plc[1]	811,640	0.3	444,350	367,290	0.1
The Burton Daily Mail Limited[1]	1,623,280	0.6	740,583	882,697	0.3
Bristol United Press Limited[1]	1,014,550	0.4	136,871	877,679	0.3
Century Newspapers Limited[1]					
Courier Press (Holdings) Limited[1]					
Watling Publications Limited[1]	811,640	0.3	147,473	664,167	0.2
Cumbrian Newspapers Group Limited[1]	811,640	0.3	284,345	527,295	0.2
The Daily Telegraph Limited[1] [2]	13,044,484	5.0	3,649,809	9,394,675	3.2
Eastern Counties Newspapers Group Limited[1]	1,623,280	0.6	1,481,165	142,115	0.1
East Anglian Daily Times Co. Limited[1]	1,623,280	0.6	1,481,165	142,115	0.1
Fleet Holdings plc[1] [2]					
Express Newspapers plc[1] [2]	3,246,558	1.2	813,296	2,433,262	0.8
Scottish Express Newspapers Limited[1]	811,640	0.3	740,583	71,057	0.02
South Wales Argus Limited[1]	811,640	0.3	740,583	71,057	0.02
Forman Hardy Holdings Limited[1]	1,623,280	0.6	740,583	882,697	0.3

Name	Prior to Combined Offering		Number of B Shares to be sold in the Combined Offering	After Combined Offering*	
	Number of B Shares Owned	Percent of Class**		Number of B Shares Owned	Percent of Class**
The Guardian & Manchester Evening News plc[1,2]	13,731,854	5.3	2,774,349	10,957,505	3.7
The Halifax Courier Limited[1]	811,640	0.3	556,263	255,377	0.1
Hirst, Kidd & Rennie Limited[1]	811,640	0.3	370,291	441,349	0.2
Home Counties Newspapers plc[1]	811,640	0.3	501,861	309,779	0.1
Independent Newspapers Limited[1]	1,893,826	0.7	547,484	1,346,342	0.5
International Thomson Organisation plc[1]					
Thomson Regional Newspapers Limited[1]	12,445,142	4.8	11,355,598	1,089,544	0.4
The Irish News Limited[1]	811,640	0.3	185,146	626,494	0.2
Irish Press Limited[1]	1,893,826	0.7	345,605	1,548,221	0.5
The Irish Times Limited[1]	811,640	0.3	185,146	626,494	0.2
Joseph Woodhead & Sons Limited[1]	811,640	0.3	456,237	355,403	0.1
N. L. Judah[3]	566,250	0.2	566,250	—	—
Kent Messenger Limited[1]	811,640	0.3	421,216	390,424	0.1
Liverpool Daily Post & Echo plc[1]	1,623,280	0.6	962,758	660,522	0.2
Lonrho plc					
The Observer Limited[2]	1,747,550	0.7	159,455	1,588,095	0.5
George Outram & Co. Limitedβ	1,826,188	0.7	166,630	1,659,558	0.6
Mercury Securities plc					
Swallow Investment Limited[4]	15,798,378	6.0	14,415,266	1,383,112	0.5
Warburco Nominees Limited[4]	999,998	0.4	999,998	—	—
The Midland News Association Limited					
Shropshire Star Limited[1]	811,640	0.3	147,473	664,167	0.2
Express & Star Limited[1]	811,640	0.3	147,473	664,167	0.2
M. E. Nelson[1]	679,500	0.3	679,500	—	—
North Wales Newspapers Limited[1]	811,640	0.3	547,484	264,156	0.1
Orr Pollock & Co. Limited[1]	811,640	0.3	183,972	627,668	0.2
S. Pearson & Son plc[1,2]					

Name	Prior to Combined Offering		Number of B Shares to be sold in the Combined Offering	After Combined Offering*	
	Number of B Shares Owned	Percent of Class**		Number of B Shares Owned	Percent of Class**
The Financial Times Limited[2]	1,747,550	0.7	550,051	1,197,499	0.4
Westminster Press Limited[1]	9,739,676	3.7	2,962,239	6,777,347	2.3
Portsmouth & Sunderland Newspapers plc[1]	2,976,012	1.1	1,824,948	1,151,064	0.4
Reed International plc[1 2]					
Berrows West Midlands Limited[1]	1,082,186	0.4	295,941	786,245	0.3
Essex County Newspapers Limited[1]	811,640	0.3	221,956	589,684	0.2
Mirror Group Newspapers Limited[1 2]	19,724,362	7.5	5,689,876	14,034,486	4.8
Northern Counties Newspapers Limited[1]	811,640	0.3	221,956	589,684	0.2
G. McG. Renfrew[3]	566,250	0.2	513,400	52,850	0.02
Scarborough & District Newspapers Limited[1]	811,640	0.3	250,930	560,710	0.2
Thomas Crosbie & Co. (Holdings) Limited[1]	1,623,280	0.6	407,321	1,215,959	0.4
United Newspapers plc[1]					
Blackpool Gazette & Herald Limited[1]	811,640	0.3	740,583	71,057	0.02
The Northampton Mercury Co. Limited[1]	811,640	0.3	722,068	89,572	0.03
Sheffield Newspapers Limited[1]	1,623,280	0.6	1,481,165	142,115	0.1
United Newspapers Publications Limited[1]	811,640	0.3	740,583	71,057	0.02
Yorkshire Post Newspapers Limited[1]	1,623,280	0.6	1,481,166	142,114	0.1
Yattendon Investment Trust Limited[1]	2,705,466	1.0	2,098,691	606,775	0.2

*   Assuming the US Underwriters' over-allotment option is not exercised and all shares offered pursuant to the Special Employee Offering are sold.
    See *The Combined Offering* and *Plan of Distribution*.
** To the nearest one-tenth of 1 per cent.
1   Member of PA. See *Principal Shareholders*.   2   NPA member. See *Principal Shareholders*.
3   Executive director of Reuters Holdings. Messrs Renfrew, Nelson and Judah are entitled to acquire 1,691,125,683,275 and 588,900
    additional B Shares, respectively, in exchange for the balance of their respective holdings of E Shares and E Preference Shares in Reuters Limited.
    See *Sale of Shares to Employees — Sales of Shares Prior to the Corporate Reorganisation*.
4   See Note 4 to the first table under *Principal Shareholders* for information with respect to the acquisition of such shares, 1,000,000 of which will be sold
    for the benefit of Reuters. See *The Combined Offering*.

Appendix 2

A REUTERS CHRONOLOGY

1848 – Julius Reuter leaves Germany and joins Havas News Agency in France.

1849 April – Reuter uses carrier pigeons to bridge telegraph communications gap between Aachen and Brussels.

1851 October 14 – Reuter opens his first London office, renting two small rooms at No. 1 Royal Exchange Buildings.

1855 – Gladstone repeals stamp duty on newspapers, thus opening up media market for Reuter's news services.

1856 – Reuter signs first agreements with French and German agencies, Havas and Wolff, for the exchange of stock market prices.

1858 October 8 – Reuter offers free trial news service to London press. After two weeks all except *The Times* take the full service at £30 per month.

1859 February – *The Times* publishes Reuter's scoop of Napoleon III's speech in Paris foreshadowing France's intervention in the Austro-Prussian war.

1860 – Reuter starts news service to British provincial newspapers.

1865 February 20 – Reuter floats his company on the London stock exchange: Reuter's Telegram Company incorporated with nominal capital of £250,000.

1870 January 31 – Reuters, Havas and Wolff sign first tripartite agreement giving each agency its own area of control in different parts of the world. The agreement dominates the international news network for the next forty years.

1871 September 7 – Julius de Reuter awarded barony.

1878 May – Baron Reuter retires as Managing Director of Reuter's Telegram Company, succeeded by his son, Herbert.

1883 – Reuter experiments with 'popular' news, instructing his reporters to include in their despatches reports of 'fires, explosions, floods, railway accidents, earthquakes, shipwrecks, street riots, duels, suicides, murders'.

1899 February 25 – Julius Reuter dies in Nice, France, aged eighty-three; he is buried in West Norwood cemetary, London.

1913 – Herbert Reuter establishes doomed Reuters Bank.

1915 April 18 – Herbert Reuter commits suicide following the death of his wife.

September – Roderick Jones, Reuters Manager in Cape Town, appointed Managing Director.

1916 December 11 – Jones and Mark Napier, Reuters Chairman, form small group to buy up entire Reuter shareholding, thus creating a new private company, Reuters Limited.

1919 – Mark Napier dies. Roderick Jones, now Sir Roderick, becomes main proprietor as well as Managing Director.

1923 – Reuterian service sends news and market prices in morse code by long-wave radio to Europe.

1925 December 31 – Press Association buys a controlling interest (53 per cent) in Reuters.

1930 December – Jones sells all but 1,000 of his remaining shares to the Press Association.

1934 February – New contract between Reuters and Associated Press disbands old cartel arrangement, giving both agencies freedom to sell their news services independently anywhere in the world.

1937 October – Government sets up Committee on Overseas Broadcasting under Sir Kingsley Wood.

November – Sir Roderick Jones discusses secret subsidy proposal with Prime Minister Neville Chamberlain.

1938 July – Jones finalises the secret subsidy agreement with the Treasury, Foreign Office firmly opposed to it.

September 22 – Hitler invades Sudetenland, Government begins subsidy of Reuters wireless transmissions from Leafield and Rugby.

1939 Autumn – Christopher Chancellor becomes a General Manager, Sir Roderick Jones remains Chairman.

1940 – Ministry of Information reveals that Reuters has received £64,000 'for propaganda purposes' from H.M. Government in the year since August 1939.

1941 February – Jones resigns after Haley reveals Reuters Board's discovery of the secret arrangement with the Government. Samuel Storey appointed Chairman. Discussions over new ownership structure begin.

October – Press Association agrees to sell half its Reuters shares to Newspaper Proprietors' Association.

October 22 – Commons debate Reuters sale to NPA.

October 29 – PA and NPA become joint owners. Reuters Trust established. Reuters Imperial News Service, subsidised by the Government, continues in spite of the Trust.

1944 – Christopher Chancellor takes sole charge of Reuters.

1945 January 1 – Radcliffe-Chancellor Agreement takes effect, lasting for three years.

1947 April 22 – Australian Associated Press take up Reuters shareholding.

May 12 – New Zealand Press Association takes up Reuters shareholding.

1949 February 1 – Press Trust of India buys provisionally into Reuters but sells four years later.

1951 July 11 – Reuters celebrates the centenary of its foundation in the City of London.

1953 – Reuters Trust amended.

1956 March 16 – Reuters world scoop on Kruschev's denunciation of Stalin at Soviet Party Conference.

1959 July 1 – Tony Cole succeeds Christopher Chancellor as General Manager and Editor.

1963 January 25 – Tony Cole dies.

February 13 – Gerald Long becomes General Manager.

1964 – Glen Renfrew appointed head of Reuters' newly established computer services, including a market quotation system to serve clients in UK and Europe.

1971 – President Nixon floats US dollar off fixed exchange rate; Bretton Woods Agreement collapses, currency market soars.

1973 – OPEC oil embargo makes currency trading even more volatile.

June 4 – Money Monitor launched.

1980 – Monitor refined to allow subscribers to 'talk' directly to each other, Reuters' profits begin to lift off.

1981 – Glen Renfrew takes over from Long as Chief Executive.

October – Executive Incentive Share Scheme launched.

December 9 – Renfrew announce new three-year plan including important restatement of the company's objectives. He calls for 'substantial rising profits'.

1982 Spring – Hare raises float proposal at Reuters Board meeting.

May 11 – Annual statement: profits in 1981 have quadrupled to £16 million, first dividend for forty-one years (£1.9 million) announced.

July 14 – NPA meets Reuters directors to discuss flotation prospects.

July 22 – Hare writes to PA chairman, Winfrey, outlining float proposal.

Summer – Matthews and Irvine work on float plan.

October 13 – Matthews tells Fleet Holdings AGM that NPA has been 'chivying' for a Reuters float.

1983 May 18 – Reuters New York Board meeting commissions first study on float proposal.

September 21 – Renfrew-Nelson memorandum persuades Reuters board to reject Matthews' plan to hive off Reuters economic services by floating them only.

October 22 – *Spectator* article 'The Price of Greed', draws attention to possible obstacle to float enshrined in the Trust.

November 9 – Reuters Board accepts legal advice that 1941 Trust is a shareholders' agreement only.

December 14 – Reuters Board decides to go ahead with flotation.

1984 January 27 – Commons debate the Reuters flotation.

June 5 – Reuters shares sold to the public on London and New York stock exchanges.

NOTES

Chapter One: THE GATHERING OF THE CLANS

1 Interview with Lord Marsh.
2 Interview with Gerald Long.
3 Ibid.
4 Ibid.
5 cf *Good Times Bad Times* by Harold Evans (Weidenfeld and Nicholson, 1983), p. 168.
6 cf the December 1981 issue of the agency's house magazine, *Reuter World,* which gave front page treatment to Renfrew's statement.
7 Ibid.
8 Interview with Michael Nelson.
9 The precise origin of the idea for special shares for Reuters' senior executives is unclear, though senior staff have attributed it to Glen Renfrew.
10 Interview with the Rt. Hon. Alan Hare.
11 Interview with Michael Nelson.

Chapter Two: RAIDERS OF THE LOST ARK

1 cf *Newspapers*: *The Power and The Money* by Simon Jenkins (Faber, 1979), p. 101.
2 Ibid.
3 Ibid.
4 cf *The Fall of the House of Beaverbrook* by Lewis Chester and Jonathan Fenby (Andre Deutsch, 1981).
5 Ibid, pp. 71–80.
6 Interview with Lord Matthews.

Chapter Three: ARISE, SIR RODERICK

1 cf *Reuters' Century* by Graham Storey (Max Parrish, 1951), pp. 59 and 91.
2 cf *A Life in Reuters* by Sir Roderick Jones (Hodder and Stoughton, 1951), p. 124.

3 cf *A Life in Reuters*, p. 98.
4 *Enid Bagnold's Autobiography* by Enid Bagnold (American Edition, Little Brown and Company), p. 210.
5 cf *The Boer War* by Thomas Pakenham (Weidenfeld and Nicholson; Futura edition, 1982), p. 100.
6 Interview with Dominick Jones.
7 Interview with Malcolm Graham.
8 cf *Barriers Down*, by Kent Cooper (Kennikat Press, New York: Holt Rinehard and Winston, reissued 1969), p. 142.
9 cf *A Life in Reuters*, p. 167.
10 Ibid, p. 179.
11 cf *A Life in Reuters*, p. 208.
12 Ibid, p. 215.

Chapter Four: THE EMPIRE FALTERS
1 cf *Barriers Down* p. 54 ff.
2 Ibid, p. 67.
3 Ibid, p. 231.
4 *A Life in Reuters*, p. 380.
5 Ibid, p. 451.
6 *Barriers Down*, p. 56–7.
7 Ibid, p. 99.
8 Ibid, p. 66.
9 *A Life in Reuters*, p. 327.
10 *Barriers Down*, p. 32.

Chapter Five: SECRET SUBSIDIES
1 *Reuters' Century*, p. 170.
2 Public Record Office, File FO 395/576.
3 Ibid.
4 Ibid.
5 de Zoete and Bevan quoted by the *Financial Times*, October 22, 1984.
6 cf *Girdle Round the Earth* by Hugh Barty-King (Heinemann, 1979), p. 252.
7 Public Record Office, File FO 395/576.
8 cf *Girdle Round the Earth*, p. 154, p. 291.
9 Public Record Office, File FO 395/576
10–20 Ibid.
21 cf *A Life in Reuters*, p. 463.
22 Public Record Office, File FO 395/577.
23 cf *A Life in Reuters*, p. 463.

24 Ibid, p. 459.
25 Public Record Office, File FO 395/577.
26–29 Ibid.

Chapter Six: A QUESTION OF TRUST
1 *Another Self* by James Lees-Milne (Hamish Hamilton, 1970), p. 122.
2 cf *Enid Bagnold's Autobiography*, p. 180/181, 229.
3 cf the private papers of Samuel Storey, MP, later Lord Buckton, kindly provided by his son, Sir Richard Storey.
4 Ibid.
5 Ibid.
6 Public Record Office, File FO 395/577.
7 cf Samuel Storey's papers.
8 Ibid.
9 cf *Reporter Anonymous* by George Scott (Hutchinson, 1968), ch. 14.
10 Public Record Office, File FO 395/577.
11 cf Samuel Storey's papers.
12–14 Ibid.
15 Interview with Sir Christopher Chancellor.
16 cf Samuel Storey's papers.
17 Public Record Office, File FO 395/577.
18 cf Samuel Storey's papers.
19 Interview with Dominick Jones.
20 Interview with Sir Christopher Chancellor.
21 Public Record Office, File FO 395/577.
22 cf Samuel Storey's papers.
23 Ibid.
24 Ibid.
25 cf *A Life in Reuters*, p. 470.
26 cf Samuel Storey's papers.
27 Interview with Sir Christopher Chancellor.
28 Interview with Vernon Morgan.
29 cf *Poor Dear Brendan* by Andrew Boyle (Hutchinson, 1974), p. 265.
30 cf Samuel Storey's papers.
31 Interview with Sir Christopher Chancellor.
32 cf Samuel Storey's papers.
33 Ibid.
34 Report of the Extraordinary General Meeting of the Press Association held at 85 Fleet Street on Friday, October 17, 1941.
35 Interview with Malcolm Graham.
36 cf Samuel Storey's papers.

Chapter Seven: THE PRIVATE BENEFACTOR

1 cf *The Post-War International Information Program of the United States* by Dr Arthur W. McMahan. Released by Assistant Secretary of State Mr William Benton in January 1946.

2 Speech by Christopher Chancellor at the Overseas Writers at Washington on Monday, January 26, 1946.

3 Public Record Office, File FO 395/577.

4–10 Ibid.

11 Interviews with author.

Chapter Eight: THE COMMONWEALTH IDEAL

1 Interview with author.

2 Interview with Alfred Geiringer.

3 cf *Don't Worry About The Money Now* by Sandy Gall (Hamish Hamilton, 1982), p. 2.

4 cf *Anyone Here Been Raped and Speaks English?* (Hamish Hamilton, 1981), p. 69.

5 Ibid, p. 71.

6 Papers received from Sir Christopher Chancellor.

Chapter Nine: BOOTSTRAPS

1 Interview with Sir Christopher Chancellor.

2–12 Personal experience of the authors, supplemented by interviews.

13 Interview with Robert Elphick.

Chapter Ten: INSTANT MONEY

1 Interview with Alfred Geiringer.

2 Interview with George Cromarty Bloom.

3 Interview with author.

4 Interview with Gerald Long.

5 Interview with Gerald Long.

6 Interview with Sir John Burgess.

Chapter Eleven: CARVE UP

1 Interview with Richard Winfrey.

2 Interview with author.

3 Interview with author.

4 Interview with Lord Matthews.
5 Interview with author.
6 Internal Reuters memorandum: September 21, 1983.
7 *Daily Mirror*: October 14, 1983.

Chapter Twelve: CASHING IN
1 *Daily Telegraph*: October 21, 1983.
2 *Spectator*: October 28, 1983.
3 Letter from Reuter journalists: November 19, 1983.
4 Letter from Glen Renfrew to UK and overseas staff: December 16, 1983.
5 Though the proposals for flotation were modified and amended, the fundamental options were set out by Warburgs in a long memorandum to the Reuters board on October 7, 1983.
6 *The Times*, January 10, 1984.
7 *Time* Magazine, June 11, 1984.
8 Ibid.
9 Interview with Richard Winfrey.
10 *Financial Times*: April 7, 1984.
11 Reuters executives, usually reluctant to talk about the details of the float, fall over themselves to criticise this piece of sharp, if selective reporting.

Chapter Thirteen: AFLOAT
1 UPI domestic news wire, May 4, 1985.
2 *Columbia Journalist Review*, September 1985.
3 Interview with Doon Campbell.
4 Interview with author.
5 Interview with author.

BIBLIOGRAPHY

From Pigeon Post to Wireless by Henry Collins (Hodder and Stoughton 1925)

The World of Action by Valentine Williams (Hamish Hamilton 1938)

Reuters Century by Graham Storey (Max Parrish 1951)

A Life in Reuters by Sir Roderick Jones (Hodder and Stoughton 1951)

Reporter Anonymous by George Scott (Hutchinson 1968)

Barriers Down by Kent Cooper (Kennikat Press, New York: Holt, Rinehart and Winston 1942 reissued 1969)

Another Self by James Lees-Milne (Hamish Hamilton 1970)

Poor Dear Brendan by Andrew Boyle (Hutchinson 1974)

The Power and the Money by Simon Jenkins (Faber 1979)

Enid Bagnold's Autobiography by Enid Bagnold (American Edition, Little Brown and Company)

The International News Agencies by Oliver Boyd-Barrett (Constable 1980)

Anyone here been raped and speaks English? by Edward Behr (Hamish Hamilton 1981)

The Fall of the House of Beaverbrook by Lewis Chester and Jonathan Fenby (Andre Deutsch 1981)

Don't worry about the money now by Sandy Gall (Hamish Hamilton 1982)

The Boer War by Thomas Pakenham (Weidenfeld and Nicholson – Futura edition 1982)

Good Times, Bad Times by Harold Evans (Weidenfeld and Nicholson 1983)

Girdle Round the Earth by Hugh Barty King (Heinemann 1979)

INDEX